Coach the Kid
Build the Boy
Mold the Man

The Legacy of Run and Shoot Football

Coach the Kid
Build the Boy
Mold the Man

The Legacy of Run and Shoot Football

Carolyn J. Ellison

With Foreword by Earle Bruce
Head Football Coach, Ohio State University, 1979-1987

Copyright © 2007 by Carolyn J. Ellison.

Library of Congress Control Number: 2007902139
ISBN: Hardcover   978-1-4257-8056-2
              Softcover   978-1-4257-8027-2

All rights reserved. No part of this book may be reproduced or transmitted in any form or by any means, electronic or mechanical, including photocopying, recording, or by any information storage and retrieval system, without permission in writing from the copyright owner.

This book was printed in the United States of America.

To order additional copies of this book, contact:
Xlibris Corporation
1-888-795-4274
www.Xlibris.com
Orders@Xlibris.com

Contents

Foreword by Earle Bruce 9
Acknowledgments 13

1. Coaching American Football 15
2. Boyhood 22
3. Main Street, Middletown, USA 29
4. Depression Years 38
5. The House of the Tiger 44
6. American Fighting Spirit 53
7. Character-Building Football 60
8. Contrasts in Black and White 71
9. Birth of the Lonesome Polecat 85
10. Operation Run and Shoot: The Boy Grows Up 95
11. Run and Shoot Goes to College 106
12. Baby Bucks and the Big Bowl of Roses 116
13. The Evolution of the Game 129
14. Real Winners 140
15. The Bridge Builder 148

Afterword: Footprints on the Bridge 151
Bibliography 155

To Glenn "Tiger" Ellison
and the quarterback within each of us
that he inspired

Foreword

In the history of American football, we can all remember the names of some truly great, tough, controversial coaches—name-brand coaches like Knute, Vince, Ara, Bear, Woody. All colorful personalities, all successful in their football programs, they were coaches no one would ever accuse of being mediocre or laid-back. Then there were those big-name players that come to mind . . . Johnny U, Staubach, Jim Brown, Jerry Rice, Montana, Archie Griffin . . . so many that it's tough to begin, let alone finish the list. Always favorites with the media for good reason, they remain in our memories when we think of great football.

But there were thousands of other coaches and players along the way who were not name brands—coaches at all levels of the game who would reach into each of his players one by one, finding the best the young man could give, pushing him beyond his personal limits, demanding preparation and hard work and personal responsibility on the practice field and in the game.

And there were hundreds of thousands of players who may not be particularly remembered for their football prowess, but if you ever sit down to watch a football game with one of them, you will know they are experiencing something different from the ordinary fan. They are watching the game all right, but they are also personally reliving their own football moment: the sultry days of summer practice, the rigorous training and preparation, the game-day jitters, the teammates who worked alongside them, the coach who pushed and prodded them to reach for their best. They even get together with other players years later and regale each other with old football stories—why they loved it, what they learned from it, who they became by it. They are reliving more than the mechanics of the game. There is hardly a man who will not tell you that the gridiron of American football taught him confidence, courage, teamwork, fair play, and the intensity for reaching a worthy goal, like no other venue in America's education system. These are lessons that, once learned, these men carry into life.

The story that follows is about one man whose name is not a household word but whose *legacy* is. Glenn "Tiger" Ellison created Run and Shoot football, which dramatically opened up offenses and gave birth to the wide-ranging variations of Run and Shoot, which are inherently a part of modern offensive football today at all levels. His story is an American football story for the times.

Tiger was more than just his Run and Shoot legacy to those of us who had the privilege of knowing and working with him. In his coaching, in his life, and especially in his interaction with people, he would always grab your attention and mesmerize you with his clear, vivid verbal pictures, and then some. He seemed to find a way to project the most positive position on everything he thought and did, and then some. He was helpful, wise, and understanding of those around him, and then some. Tiger's and-then-some factor was seared into his soul and branded on his brain, and you couldn't be around him without that positive intensity spilling over into your own spirit as well!

I was an assistant coach for the varsity at Ohio State University when Tiger was our freshman coach, and he molded a very special group of freshmen into a great Buckeye team in those glory years of 1968-1970. He had his freshmen so well coached that unlike previous seasons, the athletic director decided to schedule some games for them with other big schools in the area. All the assistant coaches would rush over to hear Tiger's pregame speech to the squad and return for his halftime speech, which was always the "clincher" to drive them to victory! What a motivator! I was primed and ready to run out on the field and play after those fiery speeches!

On a more personal level, I always looked forward to our weekly get-togethers as the Lunch Bunch—Tiger, Jim Jones, Esco Sarkkinen, George Chaump, and me—where any topic of conversation was fair game. In fact, there were times when the Lunch Bunch became the Brain Bunch because we solved all the problems that ever existed—in football, at OSU, in Columbus, in Washington DC, and across the whole world! Tiger was the old master at bringing us back to reality and the job at hand, reminding us that success in anything depends on loyalty, hard work, dedication, great attitude, togetherness, and a winning game plan. But we shared a lot of "laughers" along the way!

Tiger's story is about one great exemplary coach, teacher, friend, communicator, leader, and role model—an honest man who did a great job with and for young people. But his creative genius and positive will to win spawned a revolution in offensive football that has left its imprint forever on coaches, players, and the modern game ever since. The story is an inspiration for any serious fan, coach, or player at any level of the game who has an interest in experiencing what football can teach him about living a successful and fulfilling life. At a time when we so often hear about the bad-boy behavior surrounding the sport today, it might indeed be valuable to remind ourselves why we love it, what we learn from it, and who we can become by it.

Earle Bruce
Head Football Coach
Ohio State University
1979-1987

Acknowledgments

Any story about Tiger Ellison deserves to be told with all the flair of the master storyteller himself. Tiger was known in sports circles across the country as an orator extraordinaire, an inspirational speaker who was in constant demand on the speaking circuit for over forty years.

The late Paul Hornung, sports editor of the *Columbus Dispatch*, called him "the Paderewski of the podium, the Oliver Wendell Holmes of the banquet table, the Billy Graham of the gridiron . . . Tiger never let a prosaic phrase or a mundane factual account serve when he could think of a clear, vivid, colorful, and usually homespun way of saying the same thing. He knocked the Quarterback Club members and admiring coaches out of their seats time and again . . . New audiences might have gone through a puzzlement period when they weren't sure whether Tiger's flamboyant, stentorian delivery was supposed to be funny or serious. But they would soon discover it was the most successful combination in the business—a humor guy with a real message. He got their attention from the get-go, tickled their funny bone into receptiveness, and then socked it to 'em with a message that carried a powerful punch."[1]

So first, I must thank Tiger Ellison for leaving us his storytelling legacy, in four books that he authored; in his speeches, letters, and personal papers; and in the memories of personal conversations with him that are as indelible as they are treasured nuggets of wisdom from a great American educator and coach. I have called upon Tiger to help tell this story, and the reader will find his own words interlaced throughout this book—his in **boldface** type,

---

[1] Paul Hornung, the Columbus Dispatch, May 23, 1969

mine in normal type, all in the hope of creating a powerful, moving word-picture that carries a message Tiger-style. I believe he would be pleased with that approach, and the reader will develop a better sense of the intensity and character of the man and the times in which his story takes place. Times may be different now, but Tiger's principles for living, coaching, and teaching young people are timeless and universal. My thanks to Tiger for living those principles in exemplary fashion and leaving us his story.

Special thanks go to Bob Hart, who was there for the kickoff, coached from the sidelines throughout this project, and then stood in the end zone, leading the cheer and demanding we bring it home. Many of Tiger's former students and players spent time reflecting on their relationship with the coach and their experiences on and off the field. All of them are mentioned by name throughout this book. I greatly appreciate their participation in Tiger's story, every bit as much as their contributions to making one coach's life so worthwhile and rewarding. He never forgot one of them.

I also greatly appreciate the late Paul Day and Jerry Nardiello, sports editor emeritus of the *Middletown Journal*, for their years of reporting the stories of Middletown High School's sports. Many of the clippings of their editorials found their way into scrapbooks and files and have helped to fill out details of Tiger's story. Dan Humphries and Warren Johnson were always in the Press Box for the play-by-play and radio coverage and have been supportive of the project through access to the Old Jocks Club of Middletown.

My sisters, Nita Ellison Mata and Barbara Ellison Hartsook, have given endless hours of help and encouragement to make this project possible, reading and editing numerous iterations of the draft, sharing recollections and adding memories to complete the story. We have shared a cathartic experience reliving our dad's life, getting to know him all over again as mature adults.

The cover art and portraiture were created by my sister Barbara Ellison Hartsook. We are grateful for her beautiful gift of artistic expression, which can be found on her Web site, www.paintedgenerations.com.

Our thanks go to the following publishers for permission to use their copyrighted materials in this book:

Paul Hornung, the *Columbus Dispatch*, May 23, 1969

Edgar A. Guest, *Collected Verse of Edgar A. Guest*, "It Couldn't Be Done." Cutchogue, New York: Buccaneer Books, 1994

Glenn Tiger Ellison, the *Middletown Journal*, circa June 1949

Photos courtesy of the *Middletown Journal*

Jim Tressel, *What It Means to Be a Buckeye*, edited by Jeff Snook. Chicago: Triumph Books, 2003, pp. 85-86

Lou Holtz, *Wins, Losses, and Lessons*. New York: William Morrow, HarperCollins Publishers, 2006, pp. 91-92

Buckeye Sports Bulletin 9, no. 30, August, 1990

1

COACHING AMERICAN FOOTBALL

Coach, we're hiring you first as a teacher. Among your duties, we expect you to coach kids, to build boys, to mold men. We want these youngsters brought up the American way, which is a competitive way and a winning way. Winning is positive! Losing is negative! Let's be positive!

American football is an exhilarating display of athletic theater that has fascinated America's sports spectators for over a century. Even though baseball at the professional level captured the national imagination in the early 1900s, football at the high school and collegiate levels had already drawn crowds of one hundred thousand fans per week into stadiums across the country, well before Babe Ruth ever became a household legend.

As an offspring of the English game of rugby, American football is played with such speed and intensity, so much sheer muscularity and power, and with such intricate dynamics involving twenty-two moving parts set in motion with each snap of the ball that almost anything can happen on any given play. It is mesmerizing to watch. And it is hugely physical! A real man thing, giving young men a positive outlet for their youthful aggressions and giving the boy in every grown man a reminiscence of his youthful self.

In fact, it was so physical in its early years that in 1905, after more than 150 life-endangering injuries and eighteen actual deaths of players in a decade, President Teddy Roosevelt called upon Harvard, Princeton, and Yale to temper the rules of the game to factor in safety. There were many leaders in the federal government who saw that football provided youngsters with great physical conditioning, mental discipline, and an uncanny instinct for working together as a team toward a common goal—all qualities important for America's young men, who could then feed a strong military and defend America against her enemies.

But public alarm at the brutal casualties was causing an outcry for many colleges to drop their programs. So the rules were changed, and have been changing ever since, to create a balance between the physical excitement of the game's drama and the preservation of the bodily well-being of the players.

The physical aspects of the game are what most people know about football, whether they are crazy about it or not. But while fans may measure the team's success by its physical endurance and its win/loss record, any player who has ever gotten off the sidelines and into the game will tell you there is much more than that to American football. They may remember in detail the intricate moves, the force and counterforce, the thrill of the battle, the pain of the bruising injuries, the joy of brilliant execution. But the lessons learned on and off the field are the things they reflect on for the rest of their lives and talk about even years later when they get together with their buddies. When they watch the game, they are reliving those personal experiences—the preparation and training; the grueling disciplines just to get ready for game day; the sweet victories and bitter defeats; the teammates who worked alongside them; and the coach who pushed them, taught them, prepared them, led them into those bruising battles, and demanded of them peak performance every time.

For the coach, there are many aspects to measuring success, not all of which are necessarily aligned with what the alumni, fans, boosters' clubs, or the media think of the season. As a coach, of course, he deeply desires to teach those boys to play tough, competitive football; and he has a passion for instilling a positive winning philosophy, or else he's not worth working for as a player. Nobody gets all hyped up to be mediocre. The coach can only get them fired up by reaching for the best they have in them, by demanding excellence in performance—both in practice and on the field of play, and then by giving them the tools and training and game plans and decision making and leadership that will enable them to achieve success.

Great coaches consider their profession to be among the most honorable a man can choose. They speak of themselves as motivators and exemplars, setting the highest standards for themselves and their players, living those standards with a passion for life that moves young men to strive for the best deep within themselves. Joe Paterno has said that you must love teaching young people, more than just the mechanics of the game, the principles of discipline, loyalty and trust, respect for authority, the sense that if you work hard and do right things, you will be a better person and lead a successful, fulfilling life.

Bobby Bowden has said a coach had better believe deeply that through football, young men will develop character. Football requires sacrifice, and a man on the field can't be selfish because he can't succeed without those teammates around him succeeding also, regardless of race, creed, material wealth, or ethnic background.

Bo Schembechler believed the coach must have a passion for bringing out the very best in everyone around him, a passion for life that infuses in players the self-will to perform to the absolute best of their ability. No effort is too much; they must play with uncompromising spirit for something bigger than self.[2]

Coaches come in all flavors and personalities and leadership styles, but all are committed to learning and improving their own knowledge of the game and adapting their game plans to the particular strengths of the players they have to work with. All agree that a winning season by definition is winning one more game than losing, but they all love winning a lot more than that. If they are to motivate players to pour everything into it, then the win on the scoreboard provides the confidence to keep going.

High school coach Glenn "Tiger" Ellison put it this way in a speech before the 1964 meeting of the American Football Coaches Association in New York City:

Football is first in war, first in peace, first in the hearts of the American people.

Football is first in war because in a time of war, it is the finest conditioning for warfare—physically, mentally, and spiritually—that could be worked out. Sir Thomas Wintringham is a famous British military expert, one of their top military brass over there. After watching our American kids playing football American-style in the training camps of England back in the early days of World War II, Wintringham was so impressed that he wrote in the *London Times* these words: "The game of American football has more of the elements of actual combat than any activity I have ever seen in my life. It definitely should be an integral part of every military training program." When we get a concession like that from that old blue-blooded British boy, steeped in his traditions of soccer, rugby, cricket, and the playing fields of Eton, that means just one thing: Football,

---

[2] American Football Coaches Association, *The Football Coaching Bible* (Champaign, IL: Human Kinetics, 2002)

American-style, is first in war as a conditioner for warfare—physically, mentally, and spiritually.

It is first in peace because in time of peace football is the finest civilized substitute for war that you could ever devise. The fighting spirit burns bright in the human breast. It always did and it always will. You can write volumes of books denouncing it, you can preach against it from every podium in the land, you can call down the armies of the Lord to oppose it, but you will never get rid of the fighting spirit. It is here to stay. Well, three big cheers for the fighting spirit, and three big cheers for the rough and rugged sport of American football because it is our greatest fighting game! Therefore, football is first in peace as a substitute for war, to supply a basic need that cries out from deep inside every red-blooded youth in America.

It is first in the hearts of the American people because the underlying basic philosophy of the game of American football is the underlying philosophy of the American way of life. There is no shortcut to the goal line—it is root, hog, or die every step of the way. There is no shortcut in any business, any trade, any profession—it is dig, little pig, or starve to death. That is the football way, and that is the American way. Therefore, football is first in war, first in peace, and first in the hearts of the American people.

Glenn "Tiger" Ellison loved teaching young people, demanding that they challenge their own personal limits, watching them grow and excel. He believed down to his very core that no other venue in America's education system could instill the values of teamwork and personal responsibility toward a shared goal like the game of American football. He was disciplined and cerebral about the intricacies of the game, studying film over and over, learning new systems, looking for ways to improve the execution, drilling his players five hundred times on any new series before putting it into the game. He was always philosophical, positive, and determined to create the best team with the talent he was given each season. He was inspirational in painting a clear, vivid picture in the minds of his players, to tap and tie their motions on the field to the emotions in their hearts. He coached for thirty years at the high school level, and never had a losing season, in one of the country's toughest high school leagues.

Until 1958. For no apparent reason at all, the hard work and discipline and practice and inspiration were not working that year. More late-night film analysis, more practice drills, more new plays, more inspiring stories—all led to more of the same: losing games. The season was half over, and the team had no victories, four defeats, and one scoreless tie. The fans were doing what fans do: they were shouting that the old coach was over the hill and the school needed someone new. The players were walking around with their chins dragging because the scoreboard was defining them as losers, no matter how much of themselves they poured into the game. Football was supposed to be a positive experience, but losing is a negative one.

No one felt worse than the old coach, faced with his first losing season ever. Comments from fans generally didn't affect his positive punch about the game, but by midseason, his players would rather stare at the ground than look him in the eye, and he knew he was letting those good young men down. That is the worst thing a great coach can face, a violation of the trust placed in the coach by the players.

Tiger had played and coached football for so many years that he realized he had probably forgotten more than he consciously remembered about the game. At midseason in 1958, he decided he would have to dig up all those assumptions he had in the back of his mind about winning football, and he would have to challenge the conventional wisdom that he had been immersed in for so long. He would have to test every preconceived notion that he and every other coach had about the game.

He went back to the bare-bones rules of the game and discarded all other conventional wisdom. The bare bones left most of the page blank and opened up a whole new set of possibilities for playing the game of football. After several sleepless nights, the page had been filled with what some would later call the most wildly crazy idea that had ever popped forth from a possession football coach's befuddled brain! The new game plan was a wide-open offense called the Lonesome Polecat. The Polecat offense brought the '58 season back into the winning column and gave birth to the wide-ranging variations of Run and Shoot offenses used in the game ever since.

We had spent twenty-five years traveling the whole gamut of football offense—from Pop Warner's Single Wing to the Michigan Short Punt to the Sid Gilman T to the Don Faurot T to Bobby Dodd's Belly T—and had arrived lately at Woody Hayes's Pulverizing T. Through it all our motto was, "Hit 'em so hard and so often with so much that they simply cannot stand up in front of us!" This was serious football. We lifted weights all winter, ran our hearts out all spring, and dug ditches all summer to prepare for the fall grind. Then the Lonesome Polecat came and completely changed our football thinking.

Average football material in our town meant eight victories and a couple defeats in one of the nation's toughest interscholastic leagues, where the champion hardly ever went through undefeated. This was a sleepy town toward all things mediocre, but these people woke up and started shouting

when the team won more than eight games. They also woke up and started growling when the record showed more than a couple of defeats. This year half the season was gone, and we had posted no victories, four defeats, and a scoreless tie.

Our material was average, perhaps a bit better than average since we had seven regulars returning from a seven-and-three season the year before. There seemed no reason for us to be without victory. No team had ever worked more diligently than we had that year. We hit harder, we ran tougher, we sweat more, and we practiced longer than any team I had ever coached. Still we were winless at midseason. This was a crime, a sin, a shame—we knew it, felt it, hated it.

For years it had been our custom every Monday after a one-hour session in front of the locker room to throw the chalk against the ceiling and roar, "That's our problem for this week—let's get to work!" The players had always bounced to their feet and sprung from the locker room and hurled themselves into their drills. But not this year, not after losing four and tying one and winning none. They pulled themselves slowly to their feet, they dragged themselves sluggishly from the locker room, they went wearily to work. We wanted our boys to love football, but these kids were beginning to hate it.

"When the chips are down and the jig is up and there's hell to pay, *can you pay it?*" We used to bounce back from a defeat with that kind of talk, but after five games and no victories, we seemed to have lost our bounce. There was hell to pay all right, and we were behind in our payments.

If a man will picture his problem vividly in his mind, brand it on his brain, drive it into his heart, suddenly during a relaxed moment when the situation seems most hopeless, the right answer will pop. Put a demand on nature, and she will supply the need. From out of nowhere one bright fall morning popped the Lonesome Polecat, bringing us the right answer.

We forgot about work; we began to play. We quit being serious; we commenced having fun. We stopped our blood and thunder pep talks; we started telling funny stories. We laid aside our meat grinder; we took on the Lonesome Polecat. We halted our losing streak; we set into operation a winning streak that went all the way.

So ended the most soul-satisfying season this coach has ever known in thirty years of high school coaching. Our fans acted as if we had brought

them the state championship, our players once again proudly walked the streets with their heads up, and the coach began to send forth answers all over the country to questions asked by high school and college football coaches about the Lonesome Polecat offense.

The story that follows is the story of a coach who believed deeply that the backbone of a strong nation lies in how she educates her young people. He loved this country and believed America was the strongest nation on earth because her people were good and hardworking, and her constitutional democracy assured every citizen the opportunity to use that knowledge and hard work to achieve. He loved football as a great character-building game to give direction and purpose to the fighting instinct of this country's young men. His positive philosophy and creative will brought him through adversity to a winning solution. His story is an American story for the times.

2

BOYHOOD

The boy is the father to the man. You cannot bring up a boy on mush and milk—you have to throw him a little raw meat to chew on from time to time. No boy will ever be much of a man unless he is a great deal of a boy. While he is still a boy, he's got to stop being a quitter, a coward, a dirty player. While he is still a boy, he's got to start becoming a plugger, a fighter, a square shooter. It is up to those people who lead that boy—I'm talking about his mother and his father and his preacher and his scoutmaster and his coach and anybody else who has a hand in the leadership of that boy—it is up to those people to see that those wrong things are knocked out of that boy while he is still a boy and those right things are knocked into that boy while he is still a boy, or else he will never become a real man. Boyhood determines manhood—the boy is father to the man.

It's tough growing up human. We all come packaged with little needs and wants, doubts and demands, aches and energies we can hardly identify, let alone know what to do with, until we gain enough experience and understanding of what they are and how we can direct them in some useful way. Then there are all those other humans out there, needing and wanting and demanding right back at us in ways that sometimes work to our advantage, but very often not. It's tough.

But in rural Calhoun County, Mississippi, at the beginning of the 1900s, it was *really* tough growing up human. Most everybody was poor and living off the land. Work for wages was scarce, and new jobs had lots of able-bodied souls clamoring for them. Basic services were often lacking without traveling a good several miles along muddy country roads. Poverty and defeat were ever looming for almost everybody. Without taking some tough-minded initiative, working hard to further one's own situation, keeping healthy and fit to maintain strength, and grinding it out through the ebbs and flows, one could not survive this difficult environment.

And what was even worse in this part of rural America was growing up a black human in this environment, where the Southern white males had never quite forgiven the North for emasculating them in the Civil War and abolishing slavery. Their black neighbors were easy targets for the Southern white men's rage at those unknown Northern elitists, who simply did not understand how tough life was down there. And, of course, the majority of black Americans at that time lived in the South, with fewer opportunities for survival than anybody else on the human scale. The Emancipation Proclamation may have set them free, but being left "free" to survive here was in many ways more oppressive than before. Most would say that things remained that way until the 1960s, a century later, when the Civil Rights Act finally made freedom and equality for all blacks the law of the land.

But in 1911, into this environment was born little blond-haired, blue-eyed Glenn Ellison, the first child of Sam and Beatrice Donna, or B. D., Ellison. Sam was a flinty-eyed, tightly wired specimen of manhood, toughened on his childhood hard work of taming the land and construction work, such as it was. Southern pride was his mantle. He was fiercely loyal to the truth as he saw it. He was proud that he had obtained his teacher's license and was the schoolmaster at the Pilgreen School in Calhoun County. BD was the only other teacher at the school. She had been encouraged by her sister's husband, who was the superintendent of education for the county, to get her teaching license. They married in 1910.

BD and Sam cut a respectable swath in the rural community, as education was highly valued as a means to get out of the cycle of poverty. While Sam earned marginally more, BD earned $25 a month if her classroom averaged at least seventy pupils, no matter what age they were. If fewer than that showed up, she was docked to $23. But between them, they were doing quite well in a relative sense, even when Glenn came along. As the family grew in size through the coming years, Sam became a rural mail carrier to keep everybody fed and clothed.

Glenn and his siblings learned at an early age to chop wood, draw water, work the cotton fields, feed the animals on their small farm, and generally work as hard as they could to help Mom at home because she also worked at the school. But they also found great enjoyment from books and learning, with a little sibling rivalry as a goad for performance and with Mom as their schoolmarm. They were happy and innocent kids.

Years later, Glenn would tell a story about those days in Mississippi.

Mom was just the nicest, fairest person I ever knew, and she worked so hard. Pop would raise his voice or his belt and snap you into line with his steely blue eyes, so you didn't want to get into his sights and be doing something wrong. But Mom would just patiently guide you in the most positive way, sort of nudge you into thinking things through for yourself. I'd pepper her with questions on nearly everything because it seemed to me she *knew* nearly everything, until she'd finally just wave me off saying, "I just KNOW, by my NOSE, and my two big TOES!" That meant "We're done here!"

Down in Mississippi when we were little kids, we didn't have toys and things to play with, so we'd make up games. My brothers and sisters and I used to love to make Mississippi mud balls and throw them at each other. We'd grab sticks to try to smash the mud ball coming our way before it hit its target. Mom had to wash all those targets, and the one with the fewest mud splats won. It was always fun, and she'd pretend to be mad at the mud-soaked lot of us when we came in, then she'd just laugh at us! Southern laughter is done with a slow drawl, you know.

One day I was walking home when this little bitty black boy came skipping up the path the other way, just singing and smiling, having a grand old time! So I smiled and made a mud ball to throw at him. When he got close enough—splat! Right on target! His little face just dropped, and he started to bawl, then took off running like a scared rabbit. I remember being six years old and feeling about as bad as I'd ever felt in my life. I turned around to say I was sorry, but he was long gone.

When I went home, Mom noticed how sad I was and quietly said, "Whut's wrong, Gleee-un?" You know, when you speak Southern, you don't talk real fast. You sort of stretch it out there, so it has time to soak in. I told her what happened and that I knew I didn't hurt him—I mean, I didn't put a rock in the mud ball or anything, so I didn't know why he cried and ran. I also didn't know why I felt so awful. Mud ball is fun.

She said, "Way-el, let's see, you were both already muddy from the path, I 'spect, so it wunt the mud. And you dint have a rock in it, so it wunt that kinda hurt. Now what you s'pose kinda hurt that was, Glee-un?" She paused to let that soak in for a few seconds, then said, "The Injuns used to tell it, that you mus' walk a ho' mile in that little boy's moccasins, till you feel what he feels." She sent me off to chop some wood and think about it, never said anything more about it, and I have never forgotten it. I know that little boy didn't understand our game, and it sure wasn't fun for him. That picture has been clear and vivid in my mind through my whole life.

 A six-year-old child, in an environment of understanding, will work on even a complex problem until it's solved to the best of his ability. He'll keep on asking questions until he's worked it out. And because the mental energy and the struggle to find a solution were his own, he'll own the answers when they come.

 Hard work, no toys, no organized sports, these things gave the child time to think, and thinking about the consequences of his actions that day helped Glenn Ellison learn a lesson he never forgot. He learned at an early age to see a situation through the eyes of another person. Moms can be great wisdom counselors when they let the wisdom struggle to find its own existence in the mind of the child. BD Ellison was a great percolator of wisdom.

 The year young Glenn Ellison had been born, 1911, was the same year that BD's mother had passed away. Her father asked his son-in-law Sam at that time whether he could help the youngest of his children, sixteen-year-old Herbert, to find work. He was the last of BD's siblings living at home, and since her father was approaching the time when he would no longer be capable of doing physical labor, he felt Herbert was old enough to begin supporting himself.

Sam took all family responsibilities seriously. He had his father-in-law and Herbert move into his own home so BD could take over her mother's duties. It was there that Herbert would see Sam's baby sister Sybil, who came over almost every day to help BD with the youngsters. Sybil was a beautiful, smart, precocious little eleven-year-old who was the apple of everybody's eye. She was especially the apple of Herbert's eye.

Sam was a sharp observer of men's character and inclinations, a self-educated master of the male psyche, and he immediately began in earnest to find that strapping, healthy teenager some good hard work to offset any hormonal surges that might be in play. Sybil, after all, was *only* eleven!

He went into the library they kept at the school and took out a map of the country. Sam and BD both read the local Pittsboro paper, which got its news a few days late but kept them informed of the tremendous industrial expansion going on in the North. Ohio was of special interest geographically because the previous century had seen the development of a canal system that connected the Great Lakes region and all its natural resources in the North with the Ohio River on the southern border of the state. And, of course, the Ohio River connected to the Mississippi River, which meandered its way close by the Ellisons of Calhoun County.

Wherever those canals had been built, in addition to providing the means to transport people and goods north and south, industries began to spring up because the water provided the hydraulic power. There were lots of opportunities for a young man to find work in those industries.

When the railroad system began to take the lion's share of transporting men and materials around the country in the mid-1800s, the federal government had funded a transcontinental railroad to be built from the Atlantic shores to the Pacific Ocean. It just so happened that the transcontinental railroad crossed right through the beautiful and plush Ohio River Valley. Iron fabrication and steelmaking had taken off as an industry to supply material for rails and rail cars and to meet the growing demand of the emerging automobile industry. Much of that steel was made in and shipped from Southern Ohio. There were lots of opportunities for a young man to find work in those steelmaking and fabricating factories.

Yes, indeed, it certainly appeared to Sam Ellison that the Ohio River Valley was the crossroads of America, north and south, east and west. And the Ohio River Valley was definitely the place to send a strapping teenage boy and allow Sam's baby sister to grow up and become a fine young lady!

Since Sam had lived for so many years in the area, had taught many a lad how to go out and find work of various kinds (depending upon his own individual talents), and had delivered the mail to every conceivable corner of the rural community, he had many contacts, and perhaps some chits to call in. Within a week, he had arranged for his young brother-in-law to get a job on a flat-bottomed steamer heading up the Mississippi to the promised land of Southern Ohio. He had enough money saved for just such special needs that came along, so he would be able to give Herbert a start on his way.

When Sam told the young man of his plan, while there may have been an emotional pang of teenage heartbreak, Herbert's mind immediately began to run with the idea. He was extremely bright and well read. He was not a bit afraid of hard work or new ventures. He recognized the opportunity Sam was providing him. He imagined the rewards of the adventure ahead of him, confident that hard work for good wages in the growing steel industry would provide him with a respectable living. And he would be able to give his beautiful Sybil a home and a good life, if she would have him. Young Herbert had a clear, vibrant, romantic picture of his goal. He would make any sacrifice and do whatever was required of him to achieve it.

So it was that in 1911, a young teenager from Calhoun County, Mississippi, got on a steamer for the first time in his life, worked like a sweaty beast in the bowels of the coal room, and arrived even tougher, and certainly a lot dirtier, than he had ever been in his life. He stepped out onto a bustling dock in Cincinnati, Ohio, with a huge grin on his filthy face. He was going to become the best steelworker in all of Ohio. And he was going to win his lady.

He landed a low-level job at the American Rolling Mill Company, ARMCO, which had set up operations several years before that in Middletown, Ohio, just up the road from Cincinnati. It was a rapidly growing concern and needed strong young men who were willing to do an industrial strength job for decent wages. Seven years later, having worked his way up to shift foreman, and having saved the better part of his earnings, he booked a respectable passage on the railroad that ran from the North to the South. He took temporary leave from his job to return to Mississippi, and he married the young eighteen-year-old Sybil, his vision of loveliness who had never once left his mind.

Herbert never forgot his brother-in-law's fine hand in helping him achieve the first major goal of his adult life. He urged Sam to come back to Ohio with them, painting an exciting picture of the life and opportunities in the rich rolling hills of Southern Ohio. Sam had never given any thought to leaving the South of his birth, but the idea had been planted, and it percolated for a couple of years.

By 1920, the economic opportunities for improving one's station in life had not improved much in the South, while industrialization continued to proliferate in the North. Sam was a man with ambition to improve his lot, and his sons were approaching that age when they needed to go to work and help support the growing family. Those jobs were not available in Calhoun County, and the Ellison family was spinning its wheels on Mississippi mud. Sam Ellison decided to give up his two jobs, take his chances among the yanks, and pack up his wife and four young children to head for a trek into the unknown. With just the strength of their will to try it, their positive determination to make it, and their self-educated minds to lead it, the Ellison family headed for the steel mills of Middletown, Ohio.

3

MAIN STREET, MIDDLETOWN, USA

In 1920, nine-year-old Glenn Ellison was so excited about the trip up the nation's greatest waterway, the grand old Mississippi River, that he had barely been able to sleep nights. His dad had booked passage on an old packet steamer, not elegant but certainly affordable, as the family was to make its way to the Queen City of the West, that bustling and thriving river-port city of Cincinnati, Ohio. Their few possessions went into the cargo area, and they had a small cabin where they could sleep in shifts during the trip. Sam had once again arranged for work in the coal room, supplying the boilers that would produce the steam that would propel the paddles to carry them north.

Glenn had stuffed worn copies of two of his favorite books into his satchel so he could read to his little brother Tilmon on the way upriver and keep him occupied for the ten-day trip. These little boys' romantic fantasies had been born of Mark Twain, and the adventures of Tom Sawyer and Huckleberry Finn were just the perfect companions for them as they made their way to their new home.

By the time the family arrived at the departure dock and were ready to board the packet steamer, Glenn's vivid youthful imagination had transformed that belching beast into the most elegant side-wheeler ever to glide forth on the waterways of the Mississippi. He imagined such great adventure on this journey that before they even stepped foot onto the steamer, he and his brother had transformed *themselves* into Tom Sawyer leberry Finn! Tom, the older, painted a verbal fantasy for young Huck, of the gilded wood-carved salon, full of colorful and unscrupulous cardsharps who would relieve your pockets of your money as they smiled and chatted to your face. They were pretty sure they spotted the evil, wicked, mean, bad, and nasty Injun Joe getting on board, and King and Duke were right behind him.

They saw a black family waiting to board after everybody else did, with a teenage son who carried a dinted old brass horn over his shoulder like a hunting rifle. Tom thought it might be fun to ask him if he wanted to be ol' Jim, the runaway slave they were going to help get safely to freedom. But then Tom suddenly became Glenn again and decided to let the idea go because that boy might not understand their game, and perhaps it wouldn't be fun for him. As it turned out, they never did see that boy again for the duration of the trip, and they couldn't imagine where he had gotten to.

With the family on board and settled, Sam told Glenn that his mom would take care of little sisters Joyce and Nita, but Glenn would have to be responsible for Tilmon, since Sam would be working the coal room. That was perfect! The boys once more became Tom and Huck, and for the remainder of the trip they scampered into every nook and cranny that creaky old steamer had to offer, keeping out of the sights of the nasty villains! By the time they arrived in Cincinnati, the adventure had gone by all too quickly, and two young boys emerged with dust and cobwebs and spiders from every inch of that steamer's deck, exhausted by the trials of good over evil.

When they arrived at the river port of Cincinnati, the vivid fantasies of Tom and Huck rapidly faded, to be replaced with real images the likes of which no one in the Ellison family had ever imagined. They had never seen such a horde of people all in one place, all in a hurry to go somewhere else. Within one panoramic view, they saw refined people and cowboys and shore workers and real Indians; white people and black people and people with red hair; cows and pigs and horses and automobiles. It was a sight that gave them all pause as their eyes and minds tried to grasp the texture of the place they would come to know.

Ohio had been part of what was known as the Northwest Territory at the time of the Revolutionary War; and after the war, a large number of land grants were issued to the soldiers as payment for their service to the cause of freedom and as an opportunity for the fledgling government to help populate and tame the Western frontier. Cincinnati itself got its name from a great Roman general named Cincinnatus, who, like George Washington, had led his comrades into victory to save his country and then retired from power to lead a simple farmer's life. In 1920, Cincinnati still had a disproportionately large number of descendants of the Revolutionary

War, with all the pride and patriotism of a great and just cause passed down through the generations.

In pre-Civil War days, Cincinnati had also been the end of a main line for the Underground Railroad—that clandestine organization of white abolitionists, freeborn blacks, former slaves, and native Americans who provided the support, transportation, and safe houses for those blacks from the South who were willing to risk life and limb to escape the hardship of slavery and seek freedom in the North. Since the Ohio River was the boundary between the slave states and the North, Southern Ohio became home to many who were willing to fight for the promise of freedom.

Immigrants from Europe who had arrived into the port cities of the East Coast, found the crowded city life arduous and the textile factory wages oppressive. Many had worked their way west to the growing industrial areas of western Pennsylvania and Ohio looking for a better opportunity. So by 1920, as the Ellisons surveyed this city of over four hundred thousand people, they were witnessing a richly diverse demographic texture that was deeply bonded together with the common love of freedom, patriotism, the will to thrive and survive through hard work, the determination to succeed and reap the rewards of a better life for their families. There could not have been a better environment for Sam and B. D. Ellison to begin this chapter of their lives.

Brother-in-law Herbert had arranged for a large wagon to transport his Southern relatives from Cincinnati some fifty miles north to Middletown, where industry from the sprawling metropolis had been progressively moving northward along the path of the old Miami-Erie canal system. Herbert and Sybil would open their home to their relatives until they were settled and Sam had found work. Sybil was glad to have BD there, as she was pregnant with her first child, and BD so many times in Mississippi had proven herself to be a capable midwife.

Herbert had arranged for thirty-one-year-old Sam to talk with the general foreman of the sheet metal plant where he worked. They had become friends, partly because Herbert was so hardworking and smart, always coming up with new ideas for improving the quality of their products and the throughput of their mill. Also, every three years when the foreman bought himself a new automobile, Herbert would buy his old one from him. So it was that the next day Sam and Herbert jumped into the three-year-old Model T, a real Tin Lizzie, and drove off to the factory to find Sam work.

Armco was not the largest of the steel producing companies by far, but it had proven itself to be one of the most innovative and nimble, taking advantage of new ideas and new technologies for the production of lightweight sheet metal. They were also particularly insightful at understanding future product lines and capacities that would give the company strong positions in emerging markets. In 1920, Armco had banked its future on the growing automobile industry, and the embryonic but promising future expansion in home appliances. It had the best and most innovative research lab in the industry, something the larger and more conservative companies did not bother to invest in. While it was disadvantaged in its geographic location, being so far from the northern sources of iron ore and coal, it was well positioned to supply growing markets, due to forward-thinking people. Middletown had a great deal of pride in its innovative steel company, which would come to employ half the town's workers.

When Sam showed up with confidence in his gait and fire in his eyes and sinew in his tight muscular form, he was offered a job immediately and started a twelve-hour shift that night. He and Herbert worked the same shift in the years ahead. It did not take too long for Sam to save enough to put money down on a house on South Main Street, which in the decades that followed became the hub of Ellison family life.

Young Glenn and his sister Joyce, two years younger, were sent off in the fall to an ungraded elementary school. The Big War had put constraints on public education spending, which was just beginning to recover. The teacher at the school thought those two urchins from Mississippi must have very slow little minds, indeed, because they talked so slowly and with such funny little accents. However, she was soon to find out how wrong she was. Glenn and Joyce were both rated for the third grade level of study, and they would flow through the school system together from then on. Although they were two years apart in age, they were as close as twins and always loyal to the core to each other, while enjoying friendly debate and competition as honor students. They made each other smarter through those years.

After they moved into the house on Main Street, Glenn found a beautiful Baptist church just a few blocks away to the north, and it was the most magnificent church building he had ever seen, much prettier than the old wooden one down in Calhoun County. In his vivid imagination, it reminded him of a medieval castle with stained glass windows. He would go to that castle every week to listen to the preacher and the beautiful music. He found that church provided him the time to think and reflect on the purpose of his young life, and how to live it admirably.

He walked south one block from home, and found a corner grocery store for his mom. He eventually talked the old owner into letting him stock the shelves, break down cartons, carry out garbage, and help the men who wrestled big slabs of beef and pork onto hooks in the icebox. For this, he usually received eggs and produce that were getting too old to sell, and sometimes even a gingersnap or two from the big glass jars that displayed such special treats. These all went home to help feed the growing Ellison family. As he got older, he would work for the ice company that had supplied that huge icebox in that small grocery store. He cut, hoisted, and delivered the large frozen chunks to iceboxes all over Middletown.

The 1920s were prosperous times in the North, coming off victory in the Big War in Europe, and expansion of the industrial base in America. Wages for common labor had jumped from 20¢ an hour in 1913 to 46¢ in 1920. Henry Ford offered workers in his plants $5 per day, unheard of for the times, but soon affecting the wages of all workers. Higher wages meant more people were able to share in the prosperity. Women got the vote in 1920. The illiteracy rate dropped to a new low of 6 percent, as public support of education increased and more people were being taught the basics of thriving and prospering in the great American experiment. In 1923, public pressure brought about the eight-hour workday, and within five years, technology and productivity increases had more than offset the higher wage costs. And Middletown, Ohio, was becoming one of those All American cities in the making.

People had more leisure time to enjoy the newly found prosperity, and sports became a growing phenomenon in the American psyche. In the Ellison household, Babe Ruth and Big Bill Tilden and Bobby Jones and Jack Dempsey became objects of dinner discussions, as their exploits were broadcast over Sam's new radio in the living room. In 1924, Glenn heard on that same radio about a school called Notre Dame, a football coach named Knute Rockne, and four small but mighty fast and tough guys in the team's backfield, known as the Four Horsemen. That coach named Rockne said you had to work with the talents and strengths of the players you had, and his players had more speed than power. A game could not be won by focusing on what you don't have, it must be won by maximizing the strengths you do have. So Coach Knute Rockne popularized the forward pass in those football games, to go over the top of that defensive bulk in front of them, and then those Horsemen would run like mad toward the sacred goal line. Young Glenn thought the coach was pretty clever to think of that, and Knute Rockne became one of his imaginary heroes.

And that New Year's Day in 1925, as Glenn and his brother and sisters sat around the radio, they heard Coach Rockne and his Four Horsemen win a game called the Rose Bowl way out west in California, beating a team that outweighed them but couldn't outrun them. Right then and there, thirteen-year-old Glenn decided that he wanted to play football, even coach it someday if he could. He wasn't terribly big, but he was sure he could run like a Horseman. And he visualized that a run for a big bowl of roses would be great motivation. He would try to follow in Rockne's footsteps.

Glenn lettered in football, track, and wrestling from early teens all through high school. One more sister and two more brothers came along in those years, so now the sibling count was seven. Sam was earning decent wages at the mill, and was well on his way to becoming a shift foreman. The older boys found they could paint houses in the summer to earn money to support the growing family, and to help Middletown put a new face on its growing prosperity. When they were old enough, they would apply for summer work at the steel mill.

This generation of Ellisons also had their hearts and minds set on going to college, at the encouragement of their parents, so they made sure to keep their grades up and to learn as much as they could. Learning was fun for them. Glenn devoted all his time to his pursuit of sports and his favorite academic studies, excelling in history and English literature. His younger sister Joyce was the school's whiz kid at math and science. Glenn thought math and science, with their numbers and formulae, had no pulse beat like the stories of literature and history that involved people and faraway places and drama. But for some reason, Joyce seemed to find her subjects great. And since Glenn thought Joyce was great, he eventually kept his opinions to himself about her misguided choices.

In his senior year, Glenn decided to enter the Senior Oratorical Contest and make an inspirational speech. Perhaps his sister would then see that stories about people paint a verbal picture that captures emotion, whereas numbers and theories of science are dispassionate at best. He tells this story this way.

When I was in the ninth grade, I paid a kid a dollar to scratch my name from the speakers' list for Thanksgiving Assembly. I was scared half to death to make a five-minute speech. The thought of standing on a stage before a thousand classmates sent cold shivers leaping up and down my spine. I had not the slightest idea how a speech should be made. I felt that the moment I stood up and faced that high school audience I would surely faint on the spot. So I gave the boy the dollar my mother had given me to buy my lunch during the coming week. We were fairly poor people, and we sometimes went hungry, but I would rather have starved to death than make a speech.

But a year later I heard the first public speech I'd ever heard in my life, and I knew how to give a speech. Wade Miller was the principal of the high school, a short little man with a booming oratorical style. As he proceeded to make his speech, he shook a large jar half full of little white beans plus one big black walnut . . . hundreds of beans, but only one walnut. He shoved the walnut down among the beans to the bottom of the jar; but as he talked

he shook the container vigorously, and the walnut would rise to the top and nestle on the beans. Again and again, he would push the walnut to the bottom, shake that jar, and again and again, amidst the bombardment of beans, the old walnut would rise to the top! The name of his speech was, "You Cannot Keep a Good Man Down!"

And then I realized the secret: you have to paint a clear, vivid picture moving in a meaningful pattern so that it arouses an emotion that cements an idea! The big nut had a big problem: getting to the top. The odds were great: bottom of the pile, pressure, and bombardment from hundreds of beans. The result was victory: solution of the problem, arriving at the top. The effect on the audience was emotional: a feeling of exultation because the big nut solved his big problem while fighting big odds! The idea driven home was permanent: you cannot keep a good man down.

So I entered the senior contest and won first place by unanimous vote of the judges. The speech, entitled "World Peace," was only ten minutes long and conveyed a simple theme: man's inhumanity to man. I used up seven minutes of the ten painting a vivid word picture of an American doughboy during World War I, crawling on his belly through the mud, the blood, the filth, and the flies of France while stalking a young German soldier, whom he finally bayoneted to death after scuffling with him eyeball-to-eyeball. As the American soldier drove his steel blade home, he saw the light fade from the eyes of the young German, and he heard the dying soldier murmur, "Dear God, please take care of my mother."

I attribute that gold medal to a moving picture that stirred an emotion that drove home an idea, a picture of beans moving, and a big nut rising to the top! You can't keep a good man down!

A few days after Glenn had made his winning speech, Wade Miller called him to his office during study hall. Glenn assumed he was going to give him some pointers on how to make a better speech, but discovered Mr. Miller had something else in mind. He simply sat the young man down and asked him what he was going to do after graduation. Glenn explained he had always wanted to be a teacher and a coach, but times were still a bit lean for the Ellisons. Even though his dad was earning good wages at the mill, Glenn was the oldest of seven young brothers and sisters at home that needed to be clothed and fed and educated. He was not about to ask his family to sacrifice those needs for his college education.

So he had a new plan, and he thought a good one. He was going to go to Kelley Field in Texas and join the Army Air Corps. He wanted to learn to fly airplanes and become one of the best fighting men this country ever had in its service. You can't keep a good man down, and he was going to go soaring up into the skies for his country. And he would have little need for the money he earned, so he could send it home to the family.

Mr. Miller said to me, "Glenn, don't give up on your first dream too quickly. Our school system sorely needs good strong men of character, teachers and leaders who can show our young people how to strive for excellence, show them through counseling and example how to take their God given talents and put them on a path toward prosperity and personal fulfillment. Men who can inspire them, grow them, build character, lead them to become the best they can be. You are such a man.

"As far as the cost of a college education, if you are willing to commit to academic excellence, and play football, and work a couple of jobs for your board and room, we can get your tuition paid for. You can always learn to fly planes later. The education you get now will provide you a platform for a fulfilling life. I want you to think about that."

I was still just a green country boy, and I didn't know that you could go to college on scholarship. Wade Miller *was* inspiring! I went home to discuss the option with Pop that night, and he and Mom were elated with the prospect. I was going to college!

Then came the next hurdle: I must have been so inspiring while delivering my speech that my tonsils became inflamed and they had to come out. Dr. Shorty Reese was a local surgeon who went to our church, so I asked him how much that would cost me. He said, "Well, that will either be $50, or it will be nothing." I didn't have $50, so I told him I liked the nothing plan. He said, "All you have to do is tell me you will go to my alma mater, Denison College in Granville, Ohio, and you will pledge my fraternity, and the 'nothing' option is yours." This country boy was beginning to learn how these things worked.

In the fall, Glenn boarded a train and set off for a place he had never seen, bought for the price of his tonsils, and inspired by Wade Miller's intervention. He thought he was the luckiest guy in the world, and that some fine people of Middletown had handed him his destiny. He would be able to realize his dream of coaching football and teaching English. For a country boy with creative imagination, a talent for weaving inspiring stories, and a penchant for English literature and philosophy and history, Denison could not have been a better choice. Tucked in the rolling hills of Granville, Ohio, the campus of the small Baptist school had ivy-covered stone buildings that all looked like the beautiful medieval castles of history. Their football program was respectable for the school size, and Glenn would excel in academics and sports for the next four years.

4

DEPRESSION YEARS

As Glenn Ellison boarded the train that would take him east of Columbus to Granville, Ohio, and into his new college adventure, he reflected on his good fortune. He had a small satchel of clothes, $20 in his pocket, a shoebox full of Aunt Sybil's finest cookies, and three drumsticks of his mom's Southern fried chicken. But he considered himself a rich man because of the opportunity ahead of him to attend college and achieve his American dream, to become a great teacher, and to coach football like Knute Rockne. After all, Rockne had worked six years as a railroad brakeman just to earn enough tuition to attend Notre Dame. Glenn had been awarded a grant-in-aide, and while he had worked all summer painting houses in the blistering heat to provide some money toward his venture, he knew that it was also good physical preparation for the dog days of August just ahead at Denison. That gave his work purpose, and he enjoyed every minute of it.

In Middletown the remaining members of the Ellison family were also feeling optimistic, as Sam had earned his promotion to shift foreman, with a resulting raise in wages. Glenn had set an example for his younger siblings, and while they missed his being there, they all rededicated themselves to performing well in school so that they too might pursue their American dreams.

Then, just as they were enjoying the fruits of their labor, something called the Stock Market in New York crashed. Not one of them really knew what a Stock Market was, but the news on the radio spoke of it all the time as something quite important. They thought it must have been quite a dramatic sight seeing that big thing crash and all those stocks come tumbling down, because from then on, everybody could talk of nothing else. And everybody got depressed.

Joyce wrote to tell me that Pop would get blazing angry and start shouting at the radio when all they did was drone on about this Stock Market that crashed in New York. The angrier he got, the more she wondered whether he was really worried, although he never let on that he was. "We are in Ohio, the heartland of America! Why do we need to worry about those elitists in New York? There will be NO depression in the Ellison household. They are VICTIMS of their own GREED, but we are hard working MEN, and we will make it! We are going to continue to be POSITIVE, work toward our goals, educate ourselves, work at the steel factory, play football, paint houses. I want you boys to focus on that!" Figuring that she was an Ellison, too, Joyce also focused on that.

"Maybe Communists would sit around and wait for Stalin to fix that broken market, but not red-blooded Americans! Not Southern Americans! Not Ellison men! Why don't those Northern boys just fix it?" He really hated the Communists, and he would often rage on about those Northern moneymen who were afraid of real work! He thought Stalin was stupid for stifling individual initiative, just an excuse for taking everything away from people. Why would anybody want to work hard if it didn't lead to something better for themselves and their families? And if Stalin thought the collapse of a stock market in New York meant the collapse of America, he sure didn't know any real Americans.

Pop used to always say, "The price of freedom is that you must be responsible and work for everything you get." He loved the American Constitution. And the Bill of Rights *and the responsibilities* that go with it, as he always pointed out.

But in the months and years that followed, we were all to discover that when something in New York crashes, the dust from the fallout is scattered all over the country, and even over the rest of the world. The prosperity that had been earned by working people in Middletown was eroding, and many people were in desperate straits. Some of the kids at school were going hungry. Mom made sure her kids shared what food they had with their friends who weren't getting much at home. She had planted a vegetable garden and grape arbor in the backyard right after we moved in, and now she

watched from her bedroom window at night as people helped themselves to food for their families. Jobs were disappearing, banks wouldn't let you get your money out, and worst of all, the steel factory started losing money.

Indeed the Great Depression took its toll on nearly everybody. The steel industry, which in Middletown employed half the workers of the town, was hit very hard, and was slow to recover even years later. Capital for investment in nearly everything that required steel had evaporated, and the market for steel took a precipitous dive, from 63 million tons in 1929 to 15 million in 1932. Light-rolled sheet metal for automobiles and home appliances, Armco's strong suit, faired better than heavier grades, but the industry was leaving most of its production capacity idle in the years that followed. Sam and Herbert managed their shifts by doing some shift splitting and work sharing, and coming up with ideas for reducing costs and improving quality. But many workers simply had to be let go since their machines would stand idle for months and years to come, and wages for all workers were cut drastically.

Sam and Herbert's earnings were each cut back to about $11 per week over the next few years, but at least they still had jobs, and that kept them positive and determined. They were not used to living high on the hog, and had survived difficult times before, so even though they all became a little leaner in those days, they would carry on. Glenn pondered whether he should come home and put college on hold for a while, but Sam told him to stay in school. The part-time pickup jobs that had occupied his summers and after-school hours since he was a young teen were now being performed by former steelworkers. And no full-time jobs were available.

At Denison, Glenn found that at five feet eleven and 172 pounds, he was actually one of the larger players on the football team. And nobody had better conditioning or speed than he did. He joined the wrestling team, and became an All American Heavyweight Champion. He ran track in the spring, to stay in shape for the fall season. His summers back in Middletown offered few opportunities to work for wages, so he and his brother Tilmon did painting and handyman work without pay for those who needed the help. People got through those depression years by helping each other out.

In March of his sophomore year, when reporting to one of his two part-time jobs, Glenn learned of the tragic loss of his personal hero, Knute Rockne. After thirteen years as head coach of the Fighting Irish, with an 88 percent winning record and six National Championships, Rockne's plane on its way to Los Angeles had gone down over Kansas. At forty-three, he was about the same age as his own father, and Glenn was shattered as though he had lost a loved one. A nation of sports fans, coaches, and players felt the same way. As Will Rodgers said at the time, "Notre Dame was your address, but every gridiron in America was your home." Glenn knew that a good man had gone down.

When he returned to Denison in August of his junior year, the practice sessions during the blistering hot dog days of late summer rewarded him with a starting position as linebacker on the varsity team. He was about to meet Woody Hayes for the first time.

We were scrimmaging against the incoming freshmen scout team to get ready for our season opener. Woody, two years younger and twenty-five pounds heavier than I, had been assigned to block the linebacker. I was the linebacker. At the snap of the ball I saw this ferocious buffalo come charging at me hell bent for election. I wasn't going to just stand there and take a direct hit from all 200 pounds of thunder coming my way, so I cleverly sidestepped him at the last second and made a move to throw him to the ground. But he made a quick adjustment and instead of finding pads, I whopped him upside the head. It made a crisp cracking sound like a crochet ball being smacked by a mighty mallet.

That raging buffalo went thudding to the ground and with lightning speed rebounded to his feet and POW! He socked me with his wicked southpaw! We got into it pretty good, until our coach George Rich got us apart and demanded that we shake hands and get back to work. Woody snarled, "I'll not shake hands with that guy because he hit me upside the head!" I snarled back, "I'll not shake hands with that guy because it was an honest mistake!" Coach Rich was not buying any of it and snarled, "I'll not have dissension on my team! Hit the showers!"

I turned steaming mad and at a brisk pace headed for the field house. Pretty soon I heard buffalo hooves closing in on me, and the guy said, "Hi, I'm Woody Hayes," and he shook my hand just as nice as could be. I could never get over how a raging bull could turn into such a pleasant pup in about twenty seconds. We became best of friends for a lifetime.

Woody and Glenn discovered they had a great deal in common—coming from small towns and parent educators; being avid readers of history, philosophy, and English literature; loving football; and aspiring to become great coaches like Rockne. There were also some differences that they would learn about each other through the coming years. For one thing,

Glenn did not have that twenty-second flash point of blinding rage that in the years ahead would eventually cost a great coach his job and bring to an end a great era in Ohio State football.

When Glenn graduated in 1933, he had several offers to coach in Ohio, and an offer to become director of Physical Education at the American University in India. But when his high school coach Elmo Lingrel suggested he wanted him to be his line coach in Middletown, there was hardly any decision to make. Middletown had provided the opportunity for his father and uncle to pull themselves up from the poverty of rural Mississippi. The steel mill was slowly beginning to recover from the depression years, gradually bringing its idle capacity back online, and the people of the town were beginning to breathe a little easier. His family was there, and he would have a hand in helping them out. Middletown was home, and Middletown was where Glenn wanted to teach English and coach football American-style.

5

THE HOUSE OF THE TIGER

Middletown, Ohio, was a town beginning to feel growing optimism as it slowly began to recover from the depression, with a population richly diverse in background but inherently connected around hard work, industry, initiative, and innovation. Glenn Ellison was a man full of optimism about teaching the sons and daughters of Middletown's working class people. He was determined to accelerate their growth and make them love learning. He spent his summer days painting and fixing houses. But his evenings were devoted to developing his goals and plans for his classes, and catching up on Elmo Lingrel's football program as it had evolved over the previous four years. Football was always evolving, taking on new refinements, and good coaches were always learning from each other at clinics in the off-season. Elmo Lingrel was a great coach and mentor, and Glenn was going to be the best assistant coach Middletown could have.

He desired more than anything to make a positive difference in the lives of his students and players, to set high expectations for them and then guide them along the way toward the best performance they had in them. He would have to get their attention because not much new can be learned by those operating on automatic pilot. He wanted to engage their higher creative energies and get them involved and inspired to think, learn, and act. That overarching philosophy would underpin his coaching and teaching every bit as much as it did his own life. The specific goals along the way, and the game plan for getting there, would be different for the classroom versus the football field, but the philosophy would consistently endure.

In planning for his English classes, Glenn decided to make poetry and drama come alive through moving visual images. He had seen many a young student at Denison wince at the thought of reading a poem out loud before the class, even after the professor had given a thoughtful and thorough lecture on the clever brilliance of iambic pentameter. He would not come at poetry that way. He would recite several poems to them and ask them to listen for the drumbeat in it and to tap the drumbeat out on their desks. That drumbeat was a pulse beat that gave it excitement, a heartbeat that made poetry come alive! Lub DUB! Lub DUB! Every DUB had motion and emotion that brought excitement to the literary form called poetry. He could always introduce the old "iambic pentameter" by its highbrow Latin name at a later time.

He would tell funny little action-filled stories about Clod Shagnasty, the evil villain; and Suzey McGoozie, the dainty damsel in distress; and Dandy Doogood, the hero who against mighty odds would cleverly disrupt the wicked Shagnasty and save the damsel from her distress. Then he would assign them a classic from Hawthorne or Shakespeare whose plot would remarkably follow that of old Shagnasty and Doogood. Movement arouses curiosity, and stories at a trivial level could help the understanding of key messages on a deeper level. He would make the classics come alive.

Glenn had learned in his psychology classes at Denison that the marvelous instrument called the human brain only weighs about three pounds. That was what he had to work with in his students, three pounds of gray matter. Of that three pounds, only about five ounces are used for thinking, and the other 90% is subconscious.

You *think* with your *conscious* mind, but you *feel* with your *subconscious*, for it carries a built-in hotline that runs straight to your emotions. When you go to sleep, your conscious mind goes to sleep with you, but your subconscious never sleeps—it bobs about big-eyed and alert. When you paint clear vivid pictures in your mind during your waking hours, your subconscious looks on enthusiastically because it is forever eagerly watching. It has the *feeling*—it cannot think—that your mental screen is a television set, and the poor dumb thing loves to watch television.

When you turn off a sharp picture from your mental screen, the subconscious grabs it and absconds with it and hauls it off below the surface and stores it away in a filing cabinet. Remember, the picture must be clear and vivid. The subconscious rascal dearly loves clear, vivid pictures; it does not bother with

fuzzy ones. Later when your memory recalls that picture, the subconscious gets excited. It vibrates. It jumps up and down with enthusiasm.

Even though the subconscious cannot *think*, it certainly can *feel*; and the moment you recall that picture, bells ring and horns blow down there below the surface and the word goes out that there is an exciting show on television up above. The subconscious then does two things as it watches the show eagerly. First, it grabs old pictures from the past that it has stored away in its filing cabinet and pops them up as suggestions on how to improve the picture now showing. Second, it sends the adrenal glands into overtime, causing the adrenal glands to squirt into the bloodstream for boundless energy to keep the show on the road.

So as August loomed on the horizon and the dog days of late summer practice approached, Glenn thought about how to take his philosophy onto the practice field and get the show on the road for his first day of coaching. He knew those boys who came out for football were not afraid of hitting or being hit physically, or else they would not be there trying out for the football team. But he wanted to reach them in their hearts and motivate them. Hitting physically without purpose could be done in a bar room brawl. He needed to paint a picture in their hearts that would give them purpose on the field.

On that first day at Lincoln field, he filled his lungs full of the hot summer air and blew the screeching whistle so full of purpose that the whole neighborhood could hear it. It was about 105 degrees in the shade that day, but he thought his linemen looked sluggish as they went through their drills. With his booming baritone he began.

Okay, you puny pack of pilgrims, let me tell you how we are going to play football at Middletown High School. This is a fine town, a red-blooded all-American town full of hardworking determined people. WE are their football team. We will give those fine people every ounce of energy we have to give, in practice and on game night because they deserve nothing less. We will make them PROUD! *Preparation* **will give you** *confidence!* *Practice* **will give you** *courage!* **The people of Middletown who** *believe in you* **will give you** *cause!*

This line will work *tougher,* **work** *smarter,* **work** *harder,* **than any team in this state. I want to see you pour everything you've got into it! We hit, we block, we create space for the backfield on this team. When you see those defenders on the other side of the ball, your job is to** *sock* **it to them,** *knock* **them down,** *hit!* **And when they get back up, you s***ock it to them again, knock* *them down again, Hit! Dig, little pig! Root, hog, or starve to death!* **Now let's get to work!**

When he turned to start the drills, he realized that the more mild-mannered Coach Lingrel had stopped practice for the backs, and they were listening to his pep talk. They started cheering and applauding, and fullback Spec McGraw yelled out, *"Heyyy, Go! Tiger man! Give 'em hell!"*

Unbeknownst to Spec McGraw, in the Far East, the Tiger is the symbol of a vigorous and daring personality, one whose passion for life is contagious. His dynamic nature arouses every emotion in those around him, and indifference is not in his character. He is always primed to blaze new trails, meet new challenges, and audaciously run by obstacles that others might find prohibitive. His unquenchable thirst for life and positive action can overload the circuits of more timid souls.[3] Spec McGraw may not have realized it at the time, but he had just planted an appropriate identity tag on the coach that would follow him for the rest of his life. From then on he was Tiger, and "Heyyy! Go!" became his signature battle cry.

Tiger loved that group of guys, not so much younger than he was but all working hard and maturing in front of his eyes. Feeling confident himself, he then turned his attention to how he would teach creative writing to his English class. That particular literary form would require the students to get their most creative story-telling juices flowing. He needed to reach 100 percent of their brain capacity, to get their rational mind to organize the components of a story, but their subconscious mind actively engaged in supplying the creative juices.

He decided to use the familiar story of David and Goliath so the five ounces of thinking matter would not be strained in following the tale and so the fighting spirit in every one of those young people could emotionally identify with the underdog. The story also had all the elements of most short stories, a nasty villain and an unlikely hero who showed confidence, courage, and cause. He wanted their own stories to deliver vivid pictures that would capture the reader's emotions. Tiger's version of the David and Goliath story went this way.

Down from the camp of the Philistines came Goliath, ten feet tall, dressed in armor from head to foot, nothing showing except his two big eyes and his big ugly face. In his right hand he swung a thirty-pound sword. Down the hill came Goliath bellowing like a berserk bull. He stopped at the water's edge.

---

[3] Theodora Lau, *The Handbook of Chinese Horoscopes*, 4th ed (New York: HarperCollins Publishers, 2000)

Down from the camp of the Israelites came King Saul, five feet seven inches tall, dressed in armor from head to foot, nothing showing except his two little eyes and his handsome face. In the scabbard at his side swung his eight-pound sword. Down the hill came King Saul, walking very quietly. He stopped at the water's edge.

"I challenge you, King Saul, to fight me to death!" roared Goliath. "If you kill me my people shall be your slaves for life. If I kill you your people will be my slaves for life. To the death, King Saul!"

Said King Saul, "You wait right here where you are," and back he went up the hill to the camp of the Israelites, who gathered in a huddle around their leader.

"Who will kill Goliath," said Saul, "and save us all from slavery?" There was silence in the multitude. "Whoever kills Goliath shall be acclaimed our National Champion forevermore. Who will kill Goliath?" There was silence in the multitude. "Whoever kills Goliath shall have the hand of my lovely daughter Susey in marriage. Who will kill Goliath?" There was silence in the multitude.

Suddenly a small voice from the back murmured a response. "I will kill Goliath, sir," said David. Look at this kid David. He's just a youngster. He's not a soldier, he's a shepherd boy. The only reason he's here today is that he came over to bring some cheese and crackers to his three brothers who are soldiers in the King's army. He is supposed to return home right now and tend his sheep.

Now take a *really* good look at David. Here is a teenage kid in a goatskin holding a slingshot in his right hand, wiry as a jungle cat and healthy as a rock, truly, because he had spent most of his young life on the open range herding his father's sheep—a fine specimen of what a youngster should be physically—but no soldier and surely no match for the ten-foot Goliath who comes fully armed with the best weapons of war and fully seasoned with years of combat experience.

"I will kill Goliath, sir," said David. King Saul was flabbergasted. "Do you actually think you can kill Goliath, boy?" he said,

"Yes, sir, I think I can, sir, because I have a secret weapon he doesn't know about—I can throw rocks better than anybody. I practiced until I got good at it. I had to get good at it so I could keep the wolves away from my father's sheep. I think I can kill Goliath, sir."

"Boy," said King Saul, still flabbergasted, "do you really have the courage to go against that monster?"

"Oh, yes, sir, I know I have the courage because I have a cause worth fighting for: I am fighting to keep us out of slavery!" David looked at his king, he pictured his country in slavery to this brute Goliath, and he identified with king and country. He wanted to take their place and he wanted to take their part. He became king and country in his heart. He felt something deep in his heart like the point of a knife and the thing he felt was the greatest cause for action that burns in the human spirit: *survival.*

He looked up at his countrymen gathered about him and he pictured these countrymen gathered about him and worshipping at his feet with arms outstretched exclaiming: "Hail to thee, oh National Champion forever!" And David felt something deep in his heart like a morning sunrise and what he felt was the second greatest cause for action that burns in the human spirit: *recognition.*

"I have the courage, sir." He looked at the king's beautiful daughter and felt something deep in his heart like a covey of startled quail and the thing he felt was the third greatest cause for action that burns in the human spirit: *romance.*

"I will kill Goliath, sir," he said as he boldly strode down the hill toward the brook that bubbled in the sunshine. Goliath stood waiting, big and unbeatable. In David's mind glowed a clear, vivid picture of this thing he was fighting for, and in his heart burned an intense desire to fight and win.

David was ready. He bristled with purpose. He had a secret weapon that gave him confidence, and a cause that gave him courage. David was steeped in confidence, courage, and cause that gave him purpose, which explodes into action and gets things done. David was ready!

He stopped at the water's edge. He picked up several smooth stones. He fitted one into his sling and put the others into his left hand. He was prepared. David stepped into the shallow burbling water and waded across. He went to meet Goliath. Goliath didn't move. He just stood there amazed.

Goliath doubted whether his own purpose was so noble. *"Survival?* Is anybody going to think this skinny little teenager with a slingshot is a threat to my survival? Hogwash! *Recognition?* Are any of my countrymen going to want to hail me as their National Champion if I kill this young shepherd boy? Pig slop! *Romance?* Are the fine ladies of the kingdom going to want to kiss this scruffy face after I have snuffed out this youngster? Nonsense!"

Splat! David's stone struck Goliath squarely between the eyes, and both those big orbs popped forth like billiard balls. The giant tottered backward for a couple of steps. Then he teetered slowly to the left and then slowly to the right. Then he fell forward flat on his foolish face, gave three spasmodic jerks, and died as David leaped forward and plunged the big fellow's thirty-pound sword into the mammoth heart.

It was not just that little rock that killed the big bloke. It was the way the kid delivered it! He hit him in the eye and then he struck him in the heart. And that's the way I want you to tell stories in creative writing!

His English classes were so intense and dramatic that they started to become a thing of legend. By the time Christmas rolled around that first year, Coach Lingrel and Tiger and their fine young football team had polished off another winning season for the town. Sam was studying at night for his real estate broker's license so he could sell houses on his days off from the mill. Uncle Herbert had been promoted to general foreman of the processing plant, and had filed two patents for his inventions on Armco's behalf. Tiger was earning more money than he had ever earned in his life, and was able to take some of the burden off his mom and pop. Tiger loved his work so much that he could not believe they would pay him to have so much fun. At the Baptist Church on Christmas morning, when they sang Joy to the World, Glenn Tiger Ellison said a prayer of thanks for the joy in his world.

On a snowy day in January after the holidays, Uncle Herbert and Aunt Sybil dropped their two young boys off with B. D. Ellison on South Main Street, and drove across town to the Buick dealership. Armco had generously rewarded Herbert's promotion and two pending patents, and he was going out to buy the first brand new automobile he had ever had. As the old Model A Ford approached the railroad crossing to stop for the northbound B & O rolling into the station, the car hit a patch of ice and landed on the tracks. Sixteen tons of iron pushed the car down the tracks twenty-five yards before coming to a stop. Sybil was killed instantly, and Herbert's body was badly broken. He was taken to the Middletown Hospital where the doctors did what they could for him, but he would never walk again. When the hospital could do no more, he was transported to Sam's house, where his sister BD would care for him in the months ahead until he joined his beloved Sybil. Sam sold Herbert's house and put the money into a college fund for the two young nephews they would raise as their own in the coming years.

Tiger was devastated. He had loved and admired the brilliant Herbert and beautiful Sybil as the older siblings he never had. He continued to seek answers from God about why such talented and good people, just like Knute Rockne, would go down so early in their young lives. He found no answers. For the first time in his life, he knew what a great depression was. For the first time in his teaching, he had difficulty trying to motivate his students. Being positive was something that came from your being, and his was not feeling positive.

His sister Joyce finally took him aside and tried to provide him comfort through her perspective.

I wish I could remember exactly what she said because she explained it in a way that was profoundly simple, and simply profound. She told me that in her physics classes she had learned that nothing really disappears, it simply changes form, something about Albert Einstein and energy and mass. She was sure that dying from this earth simply released the good pure spirit of the soul from its earthly home and allowed it to return to the source. She told me not to regard this as a bad thing, just a sad thing for those of us who would miss their presence here.

I didn't understand her science at all, but it did make me recall from my philosophy classes how Plato and Pythagoras both viewed science and philosophy as one and the same. However it was that she said it, I gained a new insight into my own spiritual understanding that was deeper than just faith. It felt more like a certainty of belief. Albert Einstein and my sister Joyce were both pretty smart, and I got over feeling angry and asking why. Maybe math and science really did have a heartbeat after all. She got me back on track. And I vowed to get on with living because that's our job while we're here.

Tiger returned to church the following Sunday for the first time since the accident. As a part of getting on with living, he decided he would seek a date with the young woman he saw singing in the choir every week. Elsie Campbell was a fifth grade teacher at Lincoln School, having obtained her two-year teaching certificate by borrowing money from her Aunt Rose and attending college. She had a reputation for being a great teacher, and even though she was working to pay back her loan, she continued to take courses at night to earn a four-year bachelor's degree. Tiger remembered that they had actually spoken once in the cafeteria at Roosevelt School, when she had suggested he might want to get that spot of gravy off his tie, and then gave him a cheerful chuckle.

They dated in the weeks ahead, the first relationship either of them had been seriously involved in, and found that they enjoyed each other's company tremendously. Carrie Campbell suggested her daughter bring Tiger home for Sunday dinner because it seemed Elsie had taken quite a liking to this young man. He was passing gallantly over all the high hurdles of the Campbells' serious scrutiny and demanding standards, until Carrie served the angel food cake she had made for dessert. He politely asked if she had anymore of that delicious beef gravy she had served with dinner. She got it; he poured it over the cake and devoured it, and told Mrs. Campbell how delicious everything was. Tiger's gravy stories would be repeated and embellished as the green country boy's family lore developed through his lifetime. Elsie and Tiger were married three years later.

6

AMERICAN FIGHTING SPIRIT

The period between the Great Depression and the aftermath of World War II were years that saw tectonic shifts in the social, political, and economic fabric of America. Republican Herbert Hoover had run for president in 1928, with a promise of prosperity just around the corner for nearly everyone, a chicken in every pot, an automobile in every garage. Then the Great Depression hit, hurting nearly everyone and leaving an estimated thirteen million people unemployed. His unwillingness and some would say inability to tackle the problems aggressively were generally blamed for his loss of a second term in office.

However, unbeknownst to most people, Hoover had carefully cultivated his image in the years preceding the 1928 election because he did not have his party's necessary support for the nomination. As Secretary of Commerce under Calvin Coolidge, he was sent to manage the aftermath of the great Mississippi flood of 1927, a position he used to amplify his public exposure and demonstrate his leadership skills to the nation. He made sure the papers reported only positive outcomes of his leadership, although in truth there were many horrendous abuses of Southern black labor that went unreported.

During that time, he enlisted the support of Dr. Robert Russo Morton, head of the Tuskegee Institute in Alabama and a black man of considerable influence. In order to keep the solidly Republican black community from decrying their treatment, Hoover made a strongly implied commitment to Morton that if elected he would champion legislation through Congress to aid the poverty of black Americans. The Land Resettlement Act would have provided low cost loans for farmers to purchase small farms in the Mississippi Delta. That single act eventually could have lifted tens of thousands of black Americans in the South into the middle class. He never made good on his promise, and most likely never intended to. It did not happen.

When Democrat Franklin Delano Roosevelt ran against Hoover in 1932 promising a New Deal for Americans, many blacks supported him. The word had been spread through the black community of Hoover's failures. By 1936, Roosevelt had aggressively enacted legislation backing up campaign commitments, greatly benefiting the poor and destitute, and in that year, Americans overwhelmingly reelected him. And the party of Lincoln, which had become the party of Hoover, was no longer the party of America's black citizens.[4]

Roosevelt's New Deal was a social contract that dramatically escalated the role of the federal government in all aspects of people's lives, far beyond any existing interpretation of America's constitutional democracy. And it dramatically increased federal spending. However, it was not the New Deal that actually brought America out of depression. It was World War II. In 1939, American factories began retooling and ramping up to supply materials to the Allies in Europe, a constant stream of innovation and production that kept the Allies in the game.

When the Japanese attacked Pearl Harbor in December of 1941, America joined the fight against the threat of fascism in Europe and imperialism in the Pacific. Automobile plants were converted to war production in early 1942. Within a year U.S. factories produced eight million tons of ships, forty-eight thousand planes, and fifty-six thousand tanks. The next year those numbers almost doubled. It was a time when science and technology and American innovation were making huge leaps forward in production, packaging and distribution, automatic machinery and weapons, chemicals and medicine, radar and communications.[5]

Almost ten million of America's young men, black and white, would be sent into battle. America's factories desperately needed workers to meet the ever-increasing demand. An all-out campaign ensued to recruit women out of their traditional roles of cooking and cleaning, tending to the kids, and making home comfortable for their men. The government worked together with industry, the press, and women's organizations to propagate the message of women's patriotic duty to go to work, reminding them that

---

[4] John M. Barry, *Rising Tide* (New York: Touchstone, 1998)

[5] William A. Hamm, *From Colony to World Power: A History of the United States* (Boston: D. C. Heath and Company, 1947)

their husbands, brothers, and sons needed them to supply the materials for victory. Rosy the Riveter became the new feminine mystique for America's patriotic women, as women joined the workforce at rates never seen before. Thousands of women were recruited as nurses to join the military and support the troops. The unity of patriotic force was palpable.

Many Americans at home were making more money than they had ever made before, with very little to spend it on. Rationing of food, fabrics, and gasoline limited the resources available at home. Eighty-five percent of the country's steel and other metal production was going to support the war effort, so everything from automobiles to canned goods were in short supply. People saved their money and bought war bonds, did the best they could with limited supplies, made the necessary sacrifices to support their country in need, and felt patriotic and energized doing it. When the stakes were the very principles of freedom and opportunity that ensured a chance for a better life for themselves and their families, the populace united in a common cause worth fighting for. Liberty and freedom come at a cost.

When the United States entered the war in late 1941, Tiger Ellison went to Head Coach Elmo Lingrel to tell him of his intent to serve his country by enlisting in the Army Air Corps. Coach Lingrel strongly urged him not to take that step. Tiger and Elsie had two infant toddlers at home, and the head coach thought Tiger's contribution to his country was better played out on the football field, training and testing the mettle of many young men preparing for the battlefield. In truth, most young coaches from the high school and college ranks who did enter the service were given assignments at U.S. Naval and Army training facilities, to train young men for combat. Tiger's loyalty to his country started first with his loyalty to Middletown's young industrial-strength kids, so he determined to teach them well for what lay ahead. He would work at the steel mill during his summers off to help the cause.

High school and college football took on a greater following than almost any other local pastime in towns across the country. Football was the surrogate battle for the fighting spirit burning brightly in the hearts of America's proud citizens, many of whom had sons or brothers or fathers or uncles fighting life and death battles. But as the war dragged on, many colleges had to limit their football programs or shut them down altogether because they could not field a team. Their potential players were volunteering or being conscripted into the armed forces right out of high school. The National Football League at that time was a fledgling group of teams located in the large population centers of the North and the East. Television had yet to arrive on the scene to generate anything beyond local interest at the pro level. Many of the professional teams that did exist had the same problem as the colleges in finding available players. Those who did play for the pros were often recruited just to show up on game weekends because they needed to keep their regular jobs to pay the bills and support the war effort.[6]

So it was that high school football served a need for many Americans, vicariously rendering focus on the fight for America's future, and supplying the military with young men experienced in physical and mental discipline, personal responsibility and teamwork, leadership and confidence to be part of a physical contest. The tougher the young men played, the more the town folks identified. The Star Spangled Banner before each game left not one dry eye in the place. And the fans wanted winners, on the football field as much as they did on the battlefields of Europe and the open seas of the Pacific.

When the war finally came to an end in 1945, the warp of industrial expansion and the woof of New Deal programs had yielded a social fabric

---

[6] Michael MacCambridge, *America's Game* (New York: Random House, 2004)

that was stretched to the limits by war. The fabric would be forever altered. While the Allied victory brought relief and euphoria to freedom-loving people everywhere, the expectation had been established that the federal government of a grateful nation would take care of her people in times of need. Many women, rather than returning to their homes and leaving factory work to men, chose to remain in the work force. Labor unions had become emboldened to organize, and the steel industry resisted strongly. Thanks to the GI Bill, many fighting men who never before had the opportunity for a higher education went to college to try to improve their lot. Demand for quality education drove the passage of school bond issues that passed local electorates across the country. Black men who had put their lives on the line to defend freedom abroad came home with a new commitment to achieving it at home for their race. And pent-up demand for consumer goods and conveniences began to drive the postwar economy.

That same year thirty-four-year-old Tiger Ellison was promoted to head football coach at Middletown High School, as his mentor Coach Lingrel became the athletic director. After another winning season, Lingrel called him into his office and handed him a letter that had been sent by Melzo Morgan. Morgan was one of Tiger's fine linebackers who had joined the Marines right after graduation and had been sent to the Pacific theater.

(Photo courtesy of the *Middletown Journal*)

Dear Coach,

"When the chips are down and the jig is up and there's hell to pay, *can you pay it?*" Many are the times I heard you yell that around the football stadium. I used to admire the way you pounded your palm and beat those phrases into our throbbing heads. You drove us mercilessly when we were sweating out the dog days of August. Those early weeks of football practice were hell all right.

I thought I understood your message then, but Tiger, your meaning is coming in now, coming in strong and sharp and clear. There certainly was hell to pay aplenty, hell that demanded its payments in blood and flesh and human life. At first, right after the Japanese blasted our troop ship out from under us, there were seven of us, seven marines big enough even to play tackle for you, squeezed together in a little rubber raft, squeezed and twisted and tangled like so many fish worms in a can. Except that fish worms are moist and we were dry—scorched, burnt, cooked beyond well-done by that big ball of fire called the tropical Pacific sun.

Coach, this was no football field. This was no game of run and pass and block and tackle. This was no game of man against man where a determined guy could bunch his tired muscles and explode with a last-quarter effort to pound the enemy into submission. Our playing field was a million square miles of ocean that stretched north and south and east and west and crooked and sideways. Our opponent was the old devil sea that sometimes pummeled and smacked you upside the head. At other times the devil just lay there smacking its evil chops, waiting for you to cave.

Tiger, we were over matched. "The chips were down and the jig was up and there was hell to pay!" I could not frankly see how to pay it. Joe and Jim were the first to die. Then Big Pete went. We four who remained prayed the Lord's prayer and eased our dead comrades over the side. That was the fifth day.

Two days later George and Huck were gone, just disappeared. I know not how or why. No vote had been taken. I looked at Will lying there asleep. He and I were all that remained. By that time neither of us could talk. The boiled potato that used to be my reliable tongue was useless for forming words. I tried to *think* the Lord's prayer, but honestly, my brain was cooked.

I always thought a cold bottle of beer would be the ultimate for a man dying of thirst. I was wrong about that. Cool clear water was all I could hope for.

I knew I was dying. The last thing I remember was a strong man planted on the smooth surface of the roiling water, pounding his palm and roaring, "When the chips are down and the jig is up and there's hell to pay, can you pay it?" I tried to clinch my fists and respond, but I had nothing physically left to move or give. But, Coach, I wanted to keep on fighting.

They say that they found Will and me sitting on the beach snarling at each other like wild animals as we sucked the wild oranges strung out on the sand near the water's edge. I guess you would say that some of my fellow Marines paid more dearly, but thanks, Coach, for the preparation to muster my own will to win.

Your old linebacker,

Mel Morgan

Tiger's own confidence in his decision to stay in Middletown, coaching and teaching, was buoyed by Mel's letter. Mel Morgan was a real winner. Tiger was proud of all his kids who left for war as boys and returned as men, having fought for the cause of freedom. Liberty comes at a price. Sometimes it's hell.

7

CHARACTER-BUILDING FOOTBALL

After the war, all those who had predicted another slide into depression were proven wrong. America's factories had been running at full capacity to support the war effort, and people had money to buy things and a pent-up demand for all those scarcities that had been unavailable for so many years.

Tiger and Elsie bought a small house on Wilmore Drive in Middletown, where they could raise their young children in this town he loved to call home. His philosophy for coaching kids, building boys, molding men extended to the home front; only here it was adapted to growing girls. Tiger and Elsie had three daughters, who grew up loving football and poetry and literature, and thinking their dad was about twelve feet tall. One Sunday at the dinner table, amidst a discussion of poetry, one of them innocently said, "I can't!" With his fork halfway to his mouth, full of angel food cake drenched in chicken gravy, he dropped the fork onto the plate and slammed his palm down on the table. With steely blue eyes flashing, the baritone boomed forth:

> *Somebody* said that it couldn't be done,
> But he with a chuckle replied,
> That maybe it couldn't. But he would be one
> Who wouldn't say so till he'd tried.

> So he started right in with a bit of a grin
> On his face. If he worried he hid it.
> He started to sing as he tackled that thing
> That couldn't be done, and he did it.
>
> Somebody scoffed, "Oh, you'll never do that!
> At least no one ever has done it!"
> But he took off his coat and he took off his hat
> And the first thing we knew he'd begun it.
> With a lift of his chin and a bit of a grin,
> Without any doubting or "Quit it!"
> He started to sing as he tackled that thing
> That couldn't be done, and he did it.
>
> There are thousands to tell you it cannot be done.
> There are thousands to prophesy failure.
> There are thousands to point out to you one by one
> All the dangers that wait to assail you.
> But just buckle in with a bit of a grin,
> Just take off your coat and go to it.
> Just start to sing as you tackle that thing
> That cannot be done, and you'll do it![7]

Three spellbound little girls who had not blinked for the duration realized that they would never again say "I can't!" Wouldn't even think the words or entertain the concept! And they actually started to sing in three-part harmony, sang their little hearts out for about the next ten years. Tiger was a man's man and did not know much about bringing up little girls, except to teach them the can-do philosophy and work ethic his mom had taught him, and then just love them. He thought women, young or old, belonged on a pedestal of admiration because while they had brains that could be as competitive as a man's, they had that additional dimension of feminine capacity to understand life's meaning on a much deeper level. And he thought that women certainly looked better on a pedestal than any man ever could.

If he had had sons, perhaps the home scene would have been a lot more rough and tumble. His only sons would be the boys on his football and

---

[7] Edgar A. Guest, "It Couldn't Be Done" in *Collected Verse of Edgar A. Guest* (Cutchogue, New York: Buccaneer Books, 1994)

track teams and in his physical education classes. That was where the rough and tumble took place, in ways that by today's standards would appear a bit brutal. He used to tell this story about Chuck Asher, who played varsity football at Middletown in the late 1940s.

(Photo courtesy of the *Middletown Journal*)

Every time I think of Chuck Asher I also think of Eddie Forkner. They were two of the toughest players I ever coached. I recall the day back in 1947 when those two young huskies started something at Middletown High School that I later used as a morale builder for my football squad. It was a little activity they called "trading socks." Might not be what you think.

It all started one day after practice while the players were stripping down to hit the showers. Chuck backed up against the locker, patted his tight midriff muscles, and bellowed, "Anybody want to trade socks?"

"Yeah, I'll trade you socks!" answered Eddie. With a mile-wide grin he stalked over to Chuck and slammed his gnarly fist into Chuck's midsection.

"EEEEeee, wowwwww!" gasped Chuck. "Now it's my turn, baby!" Eddie took Chuck's position against the locker, and Chuck took his turn slamming back with all his might. "Trading socks" became a regular ritual with those two young studs during preseason practice sessions.

After Chuck and Eddie graduated, I decided to use "trading socks" as a morale booster when a couple of our players squared off against each other. During the dog days of August when the weather is steamy and practice demanding and tempers flaring and short fuses packed for maximum firepower, there were times players got into an old-fashioned knock-down-drag-out fistfight, teammates trying to kill each other in frustration! Well, that's definitely not good for team morale. So everybody would always jump in to pull them apart.

As coach I would say, "What are you fighting FOR?" And given a second to think about that, the next question would be, "Are you going to shake hands and forget it?" See, that first question is the one that's supposed to get them refocused on their reason for being there. But the second is to test whether they got through the first. If they shake hands, the rest of us give a big cheer and get on with it, morale restored.

However, if they refuse to shake hands, we declare a "sock trade" to be performed in the locker room right after practice. After the sock trade is a done deal, I tell them to shake hands and forget it while they are still gasping for air. Never had a single guy who didn't realize the value of shaking hands over another sock trade. Morale restored!

Chuck was offered a scholarship and went on to college and became a great leader of young people. Eddie was also offered a scholarship but chose to skip a higher education, something that was hard for me to understand. But I'll never forget those two fine football players. They possessed a true American spirit!

Football was still predominantly a game of power and strength, although new offensive options were being introduced every year, adding to the complexity of the game. With the end of World War II, battle-seasoned veterans had reentered civilian life, and 2.2 million of them took advantage of the GI Bill's educational provisions to enter college. That was a far greater number than the government planners had expected, but helped to keep unemployment from escalating once again. These men had put their lives on the line for the cause of personal freedom, and the government program offered them the only chance most of them would ever have to pursue the opportunity for a higher education. College football programs, starved for talent for several years, benefited greatly by this infusion of well-trained young men from the military. And the power of the physical game at the collegiate level escalated as a result.

The network of Ohio high school and college coaches was tight. Sid Gilman, friend and professional associate the same age as Tiger, was making innovative use of the forward pass and had introduced his version of the T-formation just down the pike at Miami University in Oxford, Ohio. Tiger admired Gilman as a "Thinking Man's Coach," because he was always studying game film and coming up with new ideas for the offense. They attended clinics together in the off-season, and in 1947 Tiger decided to start adding the T-formation to his repertoire of Single Wing plays at Middletown. The T required more skill and speed over brute strength, but was designed to yield more scoring opportunities. Ohio colleges recruited from Ohio high schools almost exclusively in those days, and players skilled in the kinds of play those college recruiters were looking for had the best chance of getting to college through a football grant-in-aide. The intensity of conditioning drills and practice also never let up, since his young men would have to compete with the intensity of military men forged on the battlefield.

That same year of 1947, Tiger was loading equipment into the lockers for the first day of tryouts in the stifling sultry heat of August, when a furious pounding threatened to tear loose the locker room door from its hinges. Tiger thought Godzilla had just returned from the battlefields of Europe and announced his arrival for football at Middletown High School—so emphatic was the thumping on the door. He pulled open the door to find a wiry, redheaded freckle-faced kid no bigger than a bed slat. You did not have to search for the fighting spirit deep inside this boy named Rocko Joslin. He wore it on his sleeves. His black glinting eyes and the scowl on his Scotch Irish freckled face flashed like a neon sign, shouting, "You wanna piece of me? Go ahead, I dare ya!" Here was confidence and courage personified; his only cause was to fight "just for the hell of it!"

Robert Joslin had earned the nickname of Rocko from another tough guy in his neighborhood on Hill Avenue by the railroad tracks, an Italian buddy he called Dago. Dago in turn named him "Rocco," which he said meant someone strong and durable, hardheaded and a fighter. Rocko wore the tag proudly, and not being a student of Italian, he spelled it "Rocko," firm in the confidence he was tough as a rock. Rocko and Dago could have been the poster boys for the tough blue-collar immigrant neighborhoods of the day, one Scotch Irish and one Italian, mowing down anybody who got in their way.

Rocko came by his fighting spirit honestly. His father, Burney, had grown up working the wheat harvests around Enid, Oklahoma, but moved to Ohio in the late 1920s to hop on the industrial bandwagon. He worked at Armco as a tool grinder in the machine shop by day, drank beer with the boys by night, and never backed down from a good fight. His mother, Mable, worked at a factory in Dayton making 50-caliber guns by day, and kept peace and compassion in the spirited household by night, as Burney could be quite bellicose. Rocko always wanted his dad to be proud of him, and his war stories in the neighborhood and the scars he left on others were how he earned his father's respect.

This skinny kid, who might have been 150 pounds soaking wet, said to me, "Tiger Ellison, the coach? Rocko Joslin, the player. Give me a uniform because I came to play football!" I told him he was early, and to wait an hour, then go down to the sophomore locker room. "Why the sophomore locker room? You've let other sophomores start on the varsity, and that's where I want to start. See this red hair? Now, you know, football is a fighting game, and this red hair means I'm a fighter, so why don't you just start me on varsity?" I knew no such thing about red hair, but I admired this little guy's spirit! I said, "If you're such a fighter, you start with the sophomores and fight your way up to the varsity!"

We had two-a-day practices in August, and after the morning session I was in the shower when Coach Harold Mason came in and said, "Tiger, come out of that shower because I have a story that will put hair on that old balding head of yours!

"This kid Joslin says to me, Coach Mason, I understand you are a fine coach, but I won't be with you long because I'm fighting my way up to the varsity! So I told the scrawny kid to throw a block on Big John Burney, who's six feet seven and goes 280 and is solid as a redwood tree. Like lightning he rammed Burney to the ground flat on his back, jumped on his chest, buried his face in the dirt and wouldn't turn him loose! I was standing there like a stupefied jackass, it happened so fast. We finally got him pulled off, but Tiger, I'm telling you the kid is like hot squirming wire, tough as nails and slippery as a snake!

"I said to him, what in the hell do you think you're doing? I'll kick you off this squad if you pull another stunt like that. He said, why don't you just kick me up to the varsity before I hurt any more of these little sophomores?" Coach Mason thought I might want to take Joslin off his hands.

So before the afternoon practice, I called Andy Roper, his Junior High School principal, and asked him if he knew this kid Joslin. "Know him? All too well, Tiger. The kid is always in a fight and always in my office, and he hates school. He flunked seventh grade and nearly flunked the eighth, but he loves to fight. When I ask him why he fights he says, oh, just for the hell of it! See, that's the problem, Tiger, he fights without a cause. He's from a rough neighborhood and I understand there's fighting going on all the time at home, and he seems to have the idea that the good Lord put men on this earth just to fight. You give that boy something to fight for, and you'll have yourself a good man."

That afternoon I told Joslin to get over and practice with the varsity. At the suggestion of my line coach Stan Lewis, I started him at right end after watching him block in the drills. He was much too small for the end position, and not particularly fast, but he could catch the football, and he had all the instincts and intensity and muscular reactions of a mountain cougar. And once he had been tapped as starting right end for the varsity, he refused to let anybody else take it away from him for three years straight.

On the first game of the season in his sophomore year, the Middletown Middies were playing Dayton Fairview, and Rocko Joslin was thrown out of the game for slugging a Dayton tackle. Tiger flashed the steely blues at him and said "Why, Rocko? Why?" Rocko said the tackle had punched him in the face and the referee had missed it, so he took matters into his own hands, it was only fair. Tiger sent him to the locker room and told him to wait there until the game was over. They were going to talk and set something straight for good.

After the game the locker room had emptied out, and Joslin came in with his coal black eyes glinting and his anger still blazing over the dirty hit. My steely blues moved to within inches of the blazing coals as the electricity arced between us. "I want you to listen and listen good, boy. I want to burn something into your brain, I want to brand it onto your heart, I want to sear it into your soul, and I never want you to forget it! You are no good to this team when you get thrown out of a game. You let your teammates down out there, and you have a responsibility to them and you failed to perform it for them. The next time somebody hits you dirty, you go ahead and get mad, but you HOLD it for twenty-five seconds. Then on the next play, you hit 'em hard as you can where it hurts them the most. Do you know where that is, Rock?"

"Yeah, I sure do! You punch 'em in the family jewels!"

"No, no, you DON'T punch 'em in the family jewels! You hit 'em where it hurts the most, on the SCOREBOARD, baby, on the scoreboard! You get that temper of yours under control, you channel your anger toward where it does the most damage to them, their teammates, their school, and you put your energy where it does the most good for you, your teammates, and your school. You're a smart-enough kid, Rocko, so YOU HIT 'EM ON THE SCOREBOARD, baby, on the scoreboard! Now let's win ourselves a state championship!"

Rocko Joslin never forgot. He demonstrated from that moment on that he had a cause worth fighting for, and it was indeed branded on his brain, burnt onto his heart, and seared into his soul. He was never thrown out of another game. His fighting spirit had found a home. At Tiger's suggestion, he stopped taking shop courses and enrolled in college preparatory studies. He started making the honor roll. His cause extended beyond the gridiron and into the classroom. The season ended with eight wins, one tie, and one loss.

In 1948, Rocko's junior year, Tiger realized he had the best team he had ever coached at Middletown, with outstanding talent at every position, and a team that had developed the collective respect and confidence to elevate their energy in execution. The sportswriters of the *Middletown Journal* took note of how the team played as one, more than any previous team they had ever seen, heaping praise on each other and moving like a well-oiled machine. In five of the eleven games that season they shut out their opponents while racking up 243 points, even using the second and third stringers, all of whom lettered that year. Each member of that team was different in personality and background, but when they came together on the practice field and on game night, they were united by an extra dose of winning spirit that made the team greater than the sum of its individual talents.

When I looked at them individually, there was no obvious reason why they gelled so well as a team, since they were all so different. For instance, Rocko Joslin at right end and Bobby Grimes at left end were a beautiful study in contrasts. Rocko started from a broken home and fought his way to the top. Bobby started from a perfect home and still had the fight in his heart to play football. Rocko flunked the seventh grade but ended up on the honor roll. Bobby started on the honor roll and never left it. Rocko played football like a man killing a snake. Bobby played football with all the grace of a gazelle. Rocko proved that a person can start from nothing and end up with everything. Bobby started with everything but never took anything for granted. Both men were great leaders and great team players. That team was special all right.

Ohio had a built-in rivalry between the powerhouse football teams of the industrial cities in the northern part of the state . . . Massillon and Canton McKinley and Toledo Waite . . . and the industrial strength teams in the South . . . Middletown and Hamilton and Portsmouth. In the eyes of the sportswriters across the state, who in those days voted for the rankings of high school teams, the Northeast always seemed to have an edge. But in 1948, going into the final game against Hamilton, the sportswriters had Middletown ranked overwhelmingly at number one. All they had to do was beat archrival Hamilton.

Middletown led that game until seconds before the final gun. They kicked off to Hamilton, and on a masterful play of deception by Boxcar Bailey and Jack "Flash" Gordon of the Hamilton receiving team, Hamilton ran the ball back seventy-five yards and won on the last play of the game. Once again, the Ohio sportswriters gave the nod to Massillon. But even in defeat, sometimes there is victory. The Middletown fans were so pleased with their team that they passed a school bond issue that year to build a brand new stadium on the south end of town.

The following year Rocko Joslin organized a group of students to form a Good Sportsmanship Club. The club held a pep rally before the season opener in 1949, which was once again to be Dayton Fairview. Rocko addressed the student body and reminded them that he had been thrown out of the first game against Dayton Fairview as a sophomore, but he had learned a few things since then. He urged the kids to welcome that ball club to their home field and not to boo but to boost them when they came out onto the field because they were guests of Middletown High School. He wanted the students to understand that the game of football was far more than a win/loss record. How they played the game reflected on the character of the whole student body.

Every kid in that auditorium came roaring to his or her feet to welcome Rocko onto the field of good sportsmanship. He was a leader worth following. He would go on to become the number one recruit for several Big Ten schools, including Ohio State, where he earned a starting position on Woody Hayes's team every year of his eligibility, captained the team his senior year, and graduated with honors.

In those three years, Middletown missed being voted number one in the state by one game each season, a disappointment to the coach. Tiger was asked to coach the South in the annual Ohio All Star game, and his consolation prize was that the South soundly defeated the North. But the state championship had eluded him.

Andy Roper called me after Rocko graduated, and congratulated me on the fine job I had done with Rocko and the team in those years. But I said to

Andy, "I promised that kid a state championship if he would bring himself around. He did more than that, he excelled on every front. But I didn't quite get my job done." Andy said, "Even in defeat, there can be great victory. You coached a kid, built a boy, and molded a very fine man, Tiger."

Tiger molded more than one fine man in those first five years as head coach at Middletown, and he gained respect around the state as a winning coach. And although he had seven job offers to coach at colleges and universities, and even at two of the large powerhouse high schools to the north, he chose to stay in Middletown because he loved the place and its people, and he loved his work, teaching and coaching its kids.

A decade and a half later, Curt Jones, his quarterback during those early years and the first in a long line of All State quarterbacks developed under Tiger's tutelage, wrote to Tiger the following:

Dear Tiger,

It has been fifteen years since I studied in your English class and played under your guidance at Middletown High School, but the memories are as indelible as if they happened yesterday: the "work, sweat, and tears" of dog days as you used to call them, the game plays and how you would snap me into line with the steely eyes if I didn't call the one you wanted, the inspiring before-game speeches that set our insides burning with desire to fight and win for the good of Middletown High. I could give you a play-by-play of every game, every huddle, every word in those three seasons.

But more than that, the messages that worked on the field of play were prescriptions for success in the adult world, and those are the most vivid memories of all. They have come to have more meaning through the years, and they have never let me down, Coach.

Since graduating from Purdue, I have become assistant principle, athletic director and head football coach at Centerville High in Indiana. But through it all I can honestly say I could never respect the teaching and coaching of any other person I've known more than I respect the words of my high school coach. You have been an inspiration, someone to coach like, someone to BE like.

I can only hope the young boys coming up can find the time to be part of the total football experience. If only they could realize now what football can do for them in the years after graduation, there would not be one boy in Middletown who would not want to be on the football team . . . a team

where you do not have any problem with prejudice or segregation, but only love and respect for each other and an intense desire to contribute to the cause of winning.

Thank you, Tiger. To me you are immortal.

Sincerely,
Curt Jones, Class of '49

8

CONTRASTS IN BLACK AND WHITE

When Tiger Ellison had first returned to Middletown in 1933, fresh out of college and eager to begin his career teaching and coaching, the school administrators assigned him to take on some of the coaching responsibilities at the junior high level for a couple of years. Middletown only had two junior high schools, Roosevelt on the eastside where all the affluent people and many of the working class people lived, and McKinley on the south end of town, where almost everyone came from working class families, and all of the town's black population lived. Tiger spent one year coaching each school's physical education, basketball and football programs, one with a totally white student population, the other with more than 50 percent black population.

The black community on the south end was a very tight-knit self-supporting group, where all the adults parented all the kids in the neighborhood, the churches were the center of the social fabric, and family values were universally shared. It was hard for any kid to fall through the cracks in this environment because everybody looked out for each other and all shared the desire for the kids to stay on the right path. Since fewer than 15 percent of the adults had been afforded the opportunity to get a high school education, they put great emphasis on the kids' getting as much education as they could. All were accustomed to hard work, often working two or three jobs just to eke out enough to support their families. The young boys were expected to work as soon as they were able, and physical education and sports in their younger years were valued as a means to get their young boys ready for the labor market, particularly for those factory jobs that required physical endurance. And since they were an oasis within the more unwelcoming environment of the larger community, they all worked together to help each other maintain a decent existence and a quiet dignity in spite of obstacles.

However, when they heard that a young coach and teacher, who had come to Middletown from rural Mississippi, was going to be leading the sports and physical education programs of their junior high, there was a visceral concern throughout the black community. Most had personally experienced, or had close relatives and friends who had experienced the searing racism of the South.

Choppy Saunders was in the eighth grade and going out for basketball on Tiger's first McKinley Junior High School team. He was an excellent athlete, as were several others from the black community, and he wondered whether any of them would have a chance to make the starting lineup under this new coach. The school's unwritten rule had always been that one black player would be allowed to start with the varsity. After the first week of rigorous and demanding practice, Tiger sat the boys down and, one by one, reviewed the strengths of each and the areas each needed to focus on for improvement. Then he picked his five starters, three of whom were black, one of whom was Choppy Saunders, and he set high expectations for them all.

A rash of conferences with various administrators ensued, and many late-night, angry, often anonymous phone calls began and did not let up for weeks. To each Tiger simply stated his principle, "I will start my best players. Period." Even Tiger's own father questioned his judgment and suggested that the guys at the steel mill were giving him a bad time over the situation. Tiger told him to pass along the principle, and then suggest to them they go back and read the Declaration of Independence and the Bill of Rights and tell him which parts they did not agree with. He was steely tough about doing his job and doing it right. They won the Junior High League Championship that year. Excellence was its own reward.

The word went out in both the black and white communities that Tiger Ellison was intense, rigorous, and demanding, but he was fair. He would not be pressured by conventional wisdom; he would lead by principle, and do what he knew best to produce winners. When Choppy Saunders said he would be leaving sports after the eighth grade to go to work and help support his family, Tiger tried to convince him to stay with athletics as part of his overall education. But the family's economic needs prevailed and Choppy did what he needed to do.

Through the years, Choppy continued to advance through school and into a successful career at Armco, through his own determination to learn and contribute as much as he could. It wasn't long before he and his wife Laverne took it upon themselves to conduct preschool programs at the Armco Colored Center, and to supply games and sports equipment for the youngsters at Douglass Park in south Middletown, spending endless hours there to make sure no child was ever without a feeling of love and belonging in his community. Years later, Choppy would be selected for city council and go on to become council president. Tiger Ellison would never forget Choppy Saunders as a leader and a real winner.

Middletown, Ohio, only had one high school, so those who wanted to earn a high school education were integrated into the classroom and onto the sports arenas well ahead of the societal change that would eventually follow. Tiger Ellison was never a political activist at any point in his life, but he was a teacher and coach who took his responsibilities seriously. He would find and demand the best of every kid under his care, pushing them to excel. Throughout his career, he treated them all with the same demanding standards of a man who knew the value of riveted attention, hard work, discipline, and preparation. He was tough on them, but excellence is indeed its own reward.

So by 1949, after Tiger had led the Southern All Star team to victory over the North, with five of his Middletown players in the starting lineup, he wrote an editorial for the *Middletown Journal* about the game and the win. Not much had changed in society's thinking since his McKinley days, so Tiger decided to use contrasts as a literary style to tell a great story and allow a great story to carry a meaningful message.

Winning the American Way
By Glenn "Tiger" Ellison

Twenty-five young men knelt in a little circle at the edge of a grassy playing field in Massillon, Ohio. These boys had been blown together by the four winds of heaven from the far reaches of the state. They had known each other for only two short weeks, yet at that moment they were banded together just as tightly as muscles of steel could bind them, with their sights set on the common goal immediately ahead.

Here was the big, raw-boned colored halfback from Hamilton squeezed tightly against the Catholic fullback from Dayton. Then there was the Jewish tackle from Steubenville rubbing elbows with the Protestant end from Middletown. Next was the backfield boy whose family had been on

relief during the Great Depression. Wedged in beside this lad was the guard whose parents had just given him a Buick convertible for graduation.

So it went, around that little circle—boys of every religion, every race, every rung on the social ladder. Black boys, white boys, rich boys, poor boys, Gentiles and Jews—all of them eager, aggressive youngsters ready to go all out for each other.

"All right, boys," said the coach as he joined the little group on the ground, "this is it! All history has been pointing toward this night. For years and years people of Northern Ohio have been reading about the football prowess of the Southern teams and have been asking themselves, 'Just how tough is that Southern brand of ball? They might have a fine program, but they aren't in the big leagues with us!'

"And for years and years the people of Southern Ohio have been hearing about the jolting juggernauts of the North and have been asking, 'Just how tough is that Northern football?' Tonight the truth will out. What the entire state of Ohio will think of our Southern football will be determined by what you boys do out there in a few moments. The greatest opportunity of our lives is staring us squarely in the face. We didn't come here to lose. We didn't come here to settle for a tie. We came here to *win!*

"Boys, the folks back home are sitting on the edge of their seats pulling for us with all their hearts because we represent them! They want us to go all the way because we represent every school and every city in all of Southern Ohio! Let's not make those folks back home sit there and sweat blood. Let's go all out and give them something to shout about! Now let's Go! Let's Fight! Let's Win!"

And, oh, how they did go! How they fought! How they won! They had known each other for only two weeks, but when it was all over, they hugged each other like lifelong bosom buddies . . . black boys, white boys, rich boys, poor boys, Jews and Gentiles.

That was the Southern Ohio All Star Team which I had the pleasure of coaching last summer.

No matter where you go in this land of the Pilgrim's Pride, wherever you find the school athlete . . . be he black or white, rich or poor, Gentile or Jew . . . you'll find a good, wholesome healthy youngster imbued with the ideal of democracy in his sport, and sportsmanship and fair play in his democracy, reflecting through it all a tremendous spirit of genuine brotherhood among his fellows. That is the football way; that is the American way.[8]

(Photo courtesy of the *Middletown Journal*)

Not all Americans had embraced this particular aspect of the American way in this period going into the 1950s, and his editorial spawned another rash of angry phone calls from folks in town who expected a different view from their white coach from Mississippi. But Tiger had grown up in poverty and challenging times, and knew down to his very fiber that the way to endure and break through was through hard work, self-discipline, and the positive determination to learn everything you could, all focused on a clear, worthwhile, winning goal.

It was Tiger's formula for making a real winner out of any kid who had the stuff to run with it. That would be the drill for every kid in his English class and any boy who came out for football at Middletown High School. And after packing the power of the Tiger personality behind it,

---

[8] Glenn Tiger Ellison, the *Middletown Journal*, circa June, 1949

the late-night phone calls eventually stopped, and no young person walked into his classroom or onto his playing field without knowing it.

In order to understand the environment of the day, we may need to remind ourselves of a few things about this period. The Jewish state of Israel had only been established in 1948, and anti-Semitism still ran high in the rest of the world, including the world of Middletown, Ohio. The military would not integrate its fighting units until 1947; in World War II the units were all segregated. Many heroes of the black Tuskegee Air Group, who fought so valiantly in that war and afterward attended major universities on the GI Bill, would later discover that the only offers they could find for corporate jobs would be as janitors, even though they had graduated with honors.[9]

From 1934 until the mid-1940s, the NFL had no black players, not because of any written rules, only by conventional wisdom and custom of the owners. Paul Brown, a friend and colleague of Tiger's who was respected as another "Thinking Man's Coach," broke with convention in the mid-1940s and recruited two black players from major universities because he was committed to fielding the best professional team he could. When that Cleveland team went to Florida in 1946 to play Miami, he had to leave his two black starters at home because Florida had a state law prohibiting black and white players from competing on the same field at the same time.

By 1948 there were a total of only four black players in the NFL. They routinely met with abusive language and cheap shots by opponents, none of which seemed to be noticed by the referees. In 1949, the Rams took the here-to-fore unprecedented step of recruiting the first black player from an all-black college, Grambling in Louisiana. Black players had to stay at different hotels and eat at different restaurants from their white teammates. Even white players who learned to love and respect these guys as friends were unable to prevail over the Jim Crow traditions they constantly ran into all over the North as well as the South.[10]

It would not be until the mid-1950s that the Supreme Court would end the racial segregation of schools, Rosa Parks would take her seat at the front of the bus, and Martin Luther King would lead the country into the painful awareness of the Negroes' plight in the South.

All of these things were well known in the black community of South Middletown. While the classrooms and sports fields of McKinley Junior High and Middletown High School were integrated, the rest of their lives were separate and, to a large extent, unequal. The only jobs for wages

---

[9] Suzanne Mettler, *Soldiers to Citizens* (New York: Oxford University Press, 2005)

[10] Michael MacCambridge, *America's Game* (New York: Random House, 2004)

available to blacks were for menial low-wage tasks, such as janitorial or domestic work, or for the dangerous jobs such as tending the open hearth at Armco. There was certainly no openly acknowledged interracial dating. When the kids ventured forth to go to a movie at one of Middletown's two theaters, they would sit in the balcony. When they got a hotdog at the Liberty Restaurant, they would order it for carryout. When they went to the high school kids' favorite hangout, Frisch's Big Boy, they would remain curbside rather than sitting inside. These were the unwritten rules for "getting along" and "knowing your place."

Within this context, Tiger's editorial was considered a blazing affront to some in the white community, and hopelessly naïve to some in the black. But Tiger had no political agenda, expertise, or intent, only a burning desire to teach all his young people how to become the best they could be, and he pursued it with a passion. His formula was the same for all: find the best they had in them, and push them to excel. He knew that the team sport of football was a great equalizer because every team member had to respect the job of every other man on the team in order to get a victory. When the time came for society to catch up with the classroom and the football field of Middletown, his kids would be ready.

(Photo courtesy of the *Middletown Journal*)

One of the more progressive things the school administration did in the early '50s was to replace the blackboards, which lined the classrooms of the school and tended to become chalky and streaky after the first use, with ergonomically correct, eye-soothing, nondusty green slate boards. When Tiger walked into his classroom on the first day of school that year, he thought they had painted the blackboards a beautiful color. He did not know ergonomic from shmirgonomic, but the new color reminded him of the beautiful turf in the new Barnitz Stadium on the south end of town. Since he tended to teach "football English" anyway, giving a big *"Go! Fight! Win!"* when David slew Goliath, and reading Silas Marner with the intensity of a school pep rally, he thought the new green boards would work out well.

Through the years, however, he had taken to punctuating the drama of the high point in creative writing, as when David unleashed his slingshot to kill Goliath, by pummeling his left paw into the blackboard with lightning speed just a millisecond before David's *Splat!* hit its target. That first year, as the blow was delivered, half a wall of green slate-turf went shattering to the ground with Goliath. The sound of shattering slate could be heard reverberating throughout the corridors and surrounding classrooms. He had no trouble getting the class's attention on that day.

In 1954, when fourteen-year-old Wesley James Jones walked into Tiger's sophomore English class, he had heard about the shattering green slate-turf story, along with many others that had become Tiger teaching lore by then, and was prepared to be more than a little intimidated by the overwhelming intensity and dynamism Tiger brought to everything he did. He was a serious-minded black kid and an excellent student, working hard to earn a college scholarship while most sophomores were still in the awkward stages of youth. One of the early English classes was on the literary form of Essay, and the assignment was to use that form to describe how to write an essay. Wesley wrote in his notes, "Write a how-to essay."

As his mother cleaned up the dishes from dinner that night, Wesley observed her carefully, and wrote an essay on "How to Wash Dishes." After he turned it in the next day, he realized his mistake, and for the next twenty-four sleepless hours agonized over getting a failing grade on his first English assignment. When Tiger returned the graded paper to him, he pulled him aside and told him he had never personally washed dishes, so he had asked his wife Elsie to check it over, and she had said it was perfect in every detail. But he had to give him an A-minus because that was not the assignment and he wanted to make sure Wesley listened more carefully to instructions on future work.

Wesley Jones was elated, and felt that for a white teacher in the midfifties, Tiger had been more than fair in encouraging and educating this black student. He listened very intently from then on, earned straight As, and found the experience personally rewarding. Wesley Jones went on to college, and taught high school for forty-three years. He employed many of the motivational and teaching techniques learned from Tiger, and is not on record as having ever shattered a single slate board, black, white, or green.

Pete Snow, by contrast, had a terrible time academically, but he was a gifted athlete and really enjoyed playing football for Tiger. In those days, the teachers had to report grades weekly for players on the interscholastic teams, to make sure they were maintaining eligibility. Tiger knew all too well the struggle Pete was having; he was his English teacher.

One day I told that lad to go get his football playbook. It was a big thick thing with a number assigned to every diagram of Xs and Os and arrows we had. I'd randomly call out a number to him, and he'd describe the play perfectly and tell me exactly what his assignment was on the play. We must have gone through thirty plays that way. He had a clear, vivid picture of his football assignments.

I finally closed the playbook and tossed the little old English book at him. "Pete, this is a tiny little book compared to the playbook. You've got to start caring about learning it. You need to love it as much as you love football. You need to brand it on your brain as the vibrant, pulsating, exciting, and vitally important thing that it is for achieving your goals.

"As a football player, you represent more than yourself. You represent the kids in your neighborhood, the team, the whole town, and they want to look up to you with respect for how you live your life. They want to know that you play by all the rules, not just on the football field but in the school room as well. They want to be just like you. When you mess up, it's a scar on your team and your community, and a huge disappointment to those kids who think of you as their hero. So I want you to dig deep, Pete, and start learning your English assignments as well as you learn your football assignments.

"A quitter never wins and a winner never quits. You aren't a quitter, Pete. Now you find a way to win at English."

Pete Snow dug in, and although the classroom would never be as comfortable a learning arena as the kinetic territory of the football field, he found himself pulling better than just passing grades. By his senior year, his football and his scholastics would earn him an opportunity to attend Kentucky State on a grant-in-aide had he so chosen.

Tiger's teams in the mid-1950s offered contrasts that would sometimes prove frustrating to the coach. With the right combination of size, speed, savvy, and spirit, he knew he could adapt his program and mold a winning team, provided the boys came together and gelled as teammates. But that was the elusive quality which some of his teams lacked, that commitment to each other and the instinct to play as one. He could see lots of individual talent, but without the magic spirit of teamwork, they would fail to come up to their collective potential. *Spirit* was Tiger's favorite S-word because spirit was the elusive quality that inspired a team to work together.

When Pete Snow's class of 1957 came into Middletown High School as sophomores and went out for football, they surely did not have the profusion of talent, size, speed, and savvy that Tiger was accustomed to feeding into his football program. But they had Spirit with a capital S. Pete loved the game, and had hands that could catch a football on the run anywhere on the field.

Then there was 135-pound J. B. Deaton, probably the poorest white kid ever to graduate from Roosevelt Junior High. JB's parents had divorced when he was three years old, and since his mother only had a third-grade education, she was only able to find work at the lowest end of the wage scale. There was never a lot of food she could put on the table for her son as he was growing up. Once he had entered school, his father would faithfully send him $20 a month for school lunches, sometimes the only meal he would have for the day. But JB had the spirit and positive attitude of a four-hundred-pound gorilla. Tiger would name him Waterbug because he could squirt through holes in the defensive line like a little inspired cockroach just showing off. And he was always positive and happy about life in general, and football in particular.

Leon Mitchell had all the talent to become the All State player he eventually became, along with an uncanny instinct for the game and the natural leadership on the field that could bring a team together. Bob Hart was not particularly fast or big, but he had the conditioning brought about by hard work as a child, and the discipline and determination not to let anything get past him. His eagle eyes and magnetic hands could snatch up a stray football just about anywhere on the field. Both Leon and Bob had been brought up in the black community with fathers who were demanding taskmasters, and had instilled the value of discipline and hard work in their sons.

As Tiger took inventory of his sophomores that year, he regretted ever coining the phrase "Puny Pack of Pilgrims," because it was taking on a whole new meaning with this crop of JVs. However, when they scrimmaged against the stronger, faster varsity team, they would always score on them and defend against the offense like men inspired. They were hungrier, and they were a cohesive team with plenty of Spirit!

When this puny pack came into their junior year, many of them earned starting positions on the varsity. They were still hungry and sensed that some of their older teammates might not have as much burning desire to win as they did, so they went all out to earn their spots. Senior Co-Captain Gary Getter remembered a half-time pep talk when they were playing in Dayton, and his team had languished in the first half, putting no points on the board. He knew the coach was frustrated with them, and he was prepared to hear some heavy-duty Tiger rage in the locker room.

You boys know what we need to do. But you are playing laid-back. You remember Eddie Merchant? Did Eddie ever play laid-back? Not once! He played every move, every play, every game with everything he had. Did Joslin or Grimes ever play laid-back? Never! These were your football heroes. They gave it everything they had. They played for their school. They played for the people back home. They played their hearts out for the kids growing up in Middletown who want heroes to look up to. Heroes don't play laid-back!

(Photo courtesy of the *Middletown Journal*)

When two strong men meet on the football field, the guy that gets hurt, the guy who gets his spirit broken, the guy who gets licked, the guy who gives up ground, is the guy who plays laid-back! The fellow who comes through with fighting colors is the fellow who keeps constantly bombarding his opponent with all his might and all his heart and NEVER lays back!

You've got what it takes. It'll take all you've got. It'll take every ounce of your energy and every spark of your spirit from the second you step onto that field until the final gun. I want to see your fighting spirit on that field! I want to see heroes worthy of the name! Now let's GO! FIGHT! WIN! AAAAY, Go!

Pete Snow vividly remembered that pep talk because Tiger grabbed him on the way out of the locker room and said:

Especially YOU, Pete! You are playing lackluster. Don't you realize you are playing for your hometown community? You are playing for the state of Ohio! You are playing for your country, the home of the free and the brave! Your mother is up there in those stands right now, and she is just bawling her eyes out! She wants you to GO! FIGHT! WIN! AAAAY, Go!

Pete went storming out of the locker room bellowing like an enraged buffalo. He had tears streaming down his face as he charged out onto the field looking for somebody to hit. They fought with everything they had, and they won. It was not until late in the fourth quarter that Pete realized they were in Dayton, and his mother was not in the stands.

Going into their senior year, this team lost three of their best players, one to a minor infraction in the classroom, one to a move out of town, and one who quit because he thought the coach was too tough on him. Only twenty-six players returned that year from the previous season. The team unanimously voted for Leon Mitchell to be their sole captain because of his natural leadership ability on the field.

Tiger knew what the sportswriters were saying about this team was probably true, that this puny pack of pilgrims would be lucky if they could win two games, since the schedule had them matched against four of the top ten teams in the state, and six of the top fifteen. But this team had fighting spirit, great leadership under Leon, and team cohesiveness that cannot be bought at any price. They won seven, lost one, and tied two. In that one loss, Tiger had sent in the call for a punt on fourth down and one yard, rather than running the ball. After the game, he told the boys they had not lost that game; the Tiger had. And he promised never to do that to them again.

Of the eight black starters on the varsity team, it was rare to have two of them recruited by the major universities in Ohio. But that year, speedy halfback John Earl Moore accepted Johnny Pont's offer to attend Miami of Ohio in Oxford. And Leon Mitchell was Woody Hayes's number one recruit for Ohio State, and he had several other big schools after him. Johnny Pont would continue to try to persuade Leon to come to Miami, even after he had decided for personal reasons that he would prefer to go to work and start earning a living at the paper mill in Middletown.

It was not unusual in the 1950s for black players to be completely overlooked by the universities with major powerhouse football programs. In the past, Eddie Merchant had been the only black player from Middletown to receive such an offer, being recruited by Ara Parseghian when he held the head coaching job at Miami four years earlier. However, the black colleges in Tennessee, Kentucky, and Virginia recruited heavily from Middletown because they knew Tiger was a demanding coach who prepared his players well for the next level.

A few players, including Bob Hart, were offered grants-in-aide at Kentucky State College, but Bob had his heart set on going to Miami, where his cousin Eddie Merchant had gone. So Bob turned down the opportunity, and instead worked three jobs for the next eighteen months, in order to earn enough money to enroll at Miami for a year and take his chances as a walk-on for Johnny Pont's team.

I didn't agree with Bobby Hart's decision to turn down a sure-thing offer to get a higher education. The college programs at the major universities were hard for a black boy to break into because Ohio high school football programs produced so many quality white boys who were vying for those scholarships. Besides, I had Hart playing tackle his senior year. He wasn't really big enough for that position, but that's where I needed him, and he did an excellent job for us. But he would have a hard time competing against some of those bigger tackles from the North. He was more cut out to be an end, but all our films showed him at tackle.

Besides, as Eddie Merchant knew from personal experience, sometimes the white teammates could make a black player's life tough. I thought the chance to go to Kentucky State was something Bob should do in order to get the higher education that would set him on a path for life. Then Elsie reminded me of something. She said, "Tiger, remember Wade Miller's speech about how you can't keep a good man down? A black walnut being pushed to the bottom of the pile, buried under hundreds of white beans? Then the jar being shaken, the walnut bombarded by all those white beans, and eventually, with enough energy and determination, the walnut rises to

the top? Well, maybe Bob Hart knows what he's doing, has a clear picture of his goal in mind, and he's a good man who can't be kept down." Elsie was pretty smart when it came to knowing people.

Bob never took his eye off his goal, even through eighteen months of low-level jobs and four hours of sleep a night. He called Tiger in the winter of 1959 and asked to stop by the house on Highview Road so they could talk for a few minutes. He had enrolled at Miami and would be going out for spring practice to try to make Pont's Redskin team, and was hoping to get a grant-in-aide. Tiger wished him the best of luck, and told him to stay in touch. Tiger called Johnny the next day just to give him a heads-up about the work ethic and positive determination of this young man. Within his first week of practice, Bob earned that scholarship and lettered as varsity offensive or defensive end every year of his eligibility. After graduation four years later, he went on to begin a highly successful management career with Ford Motor Company in Detroit.

What Bob knew that Tiger did not, was that very few major high schools or corporations recruited from the black colleges in those days. Even his cousin Eddie Merchant, after graduating from Miami, had only been offered a teaching and coaching job at the black high school of Cleveland East Tech. And although Bob had originally hoped to major in education and return to Middletown to teach history and coach football with Tiger, he realized based on Eddie's experience that such a goal was probably unattainable. So he redirected his career goals toward a corporate path. Fortunately, because the activist Congressman Adam Clayton Powell had been aggressively trying to get Henry Ford and other captains of industry to open up their companies' hiring practices to qualified black graduates, his timing was perfect in 1963 to begin a successful corporate career. He would continue throughout his lifetime to mentor and assist young people, especially the black kids in his community, to pursue their dreams.

Such were the contrasts in black and white in the late '50s.

9

BIRTH OF THE LONESOME POLECAT

Middletown, Ohio, in the late fifties was a community firmly steeped in the ways of the winner. The school was known not only for the brand of rough and rugged football it played, but was considered by most sportswriters who paid attention to those things in those days, the home of the best high school basketball team in the whole country. That was because of the outstanding ability of Coach Paul Walker to produce winners, and also the incredible talent and work ethic demanded by the working families of this industrial community. A young man by the name of Jerry Lucas had decided in Junior High that he was going to excel at basketball, every bit as much as he did at academics, and at an early age, he threw himself into the training and preparation to be the best.

Every day of every summer, this tall, lanky lad would ride his bike over to the east end's community basketball court, even when the heat waves were wafting over the concrete or the rain was pelting down, and put in a minimum of two hours practicing round ball each day. With the basketball under his arm and a big piece of chalk in his hand, he would set about drawing two-foot circles that arched around the hoop, to the left and to the right and in the front and at varying distances away from the basket, until he had a total of thirteen circles. Every day the drill was the same. He would fire from a near circle until he made ten baskets in a row. If he missed, he would follow the ball in to make the rebound and layup, and start the count to ten all over again. Day in and day out, Jerry Lucas kept methodically practicing to become a championship scoring machine from anywhere on the court.

On the south end of town there was A. C. Mitchell, who had played both football and basketball in Junior High, and during the summers when he wasn't working at odd jobs to help the family with spending money, he would head for the basketball court in Douglass Park to find a pickup game with other kids and adults of all ages who happened to be around. AC had always been a strong, natural athlete who was lightning quick on his feet and could practically spring to a four-foot vertical jump from a standing position. By the time he was ready to enter high school, however, his mother had put her foot down and insisted he give up sports. They were a poor family, and she could not afford insurance should he get injured playing.

But AC also had other natural abilities besides his athleticism, including a quick wit and the uncanny ability to be charmingly persuasive. With relentless enthusiasm, he eventually cajoled his mother into letting him at least play basketball, even though his bargaining chip had been to give up football. Through his humor and persistence, he convinced her that Coach Walker's brand of Run and Shoot basketball was 95 percent offense and very little defense, so he would not get hurt. So with Jerry Lucas consistently able to hit a basket from anywhere on the floor, and A. C. Mitchell leaping higher than anybody else under the basket to catch and dunk an incoming pass or snatch up a rebound, that high school team ran and shot its way to seventy-six straight victories for the Middletown Middies and three State Championships on the basketball court.

Tiger Ellison would have dearly loved having some of that unbridled enthusiasm and serious talent on his football teams in the late '50s. A decade earlier, he had had the best football team he had ever coached, but by the late '50s, even though the boys practiced just as hard and played just as tough, his teams lacked that spark that makes average talent good, and good talent great. The Lucas family had contributed Jerry's younger brother Roy to Tiger's football family, a kid with the same work ethic as his older brother and an All State end with great talent as a receiver. But although Tiger had always considered himself to be a pretty persuasive negotiator, for three years he had been unable to convince A. C. Mitchell to come out for his football team. AC would have loved nothing more than to put his athletic talents to work on the gridiron, but he had made a commitment to his mom and continued to honor it.

Tiger would have to settle for coaching AC and Jerry on his track team in the spring. Track was considered a conditioning rather than a competitive sport in those days, with a minimal budget resulting in old equipment and no uniforms. Jerry Lucas used shot put to maintain upper body strength conditioning, and did so well at it that in his senior year Tiger decided to pop him into his car and drive him to the regional competition. Then when AC was a senior and applied his incredible vertical leaping ability to the high jump event, he persuaded Tiger to pop *him* into that car, and take him to the regionals to compete against other high jumpers in the state. In true AC negotiating fashion, he bet the coach a chicken dinner that he would get a ribbon. Tiger admired his confidence and competitive nature, and began to view track in a new competitive light.

AC got his ribbon, so Tiger upped the ante to two chicken dinners if he placed in the state meet. He placed second in the state, the highest competitive showing Tiger had ever had with his track team. When AC came to collect, he received five chits for chicken dinners at Frisch's Big Boy, a bonanza for a poor kid from the south end.

Jerry Lucas would go on to play varsity basketball for Ohio State University, graduate with honors, and contribute to some glory years for the New York Knicks in the ten years that followed. AC would go to work at Armco right out of high school to help support his mother, and later he would mentor and coach the young people in his community, and become an active member of the Middletown School Board for twelve years. Both men were great competitors and real winners in the game of life.

By the end of the 1950s, professional football had begun to overtake baseball as the national pastime, as the NFL had come into its own on a national scale. Twenty-five million television sets in American homes had brought more people into the excitement of the game than ever before. *Sports Illustrated* began publishing in the mid-1950s to help serious fans become more knowledgeable and conversant with the intricacies of the game of American football. Paul Brown in Cleveland, Weeb Eubank in Baltimore, and Sid Gilman in Los Angeles, all Ohio coaches whom Tiger knew very well and followed very closely, were opening up their offenses and turning their teams into professional fan pleasers. Vince Lombardi and Tom Landry in New York were turning their New York bunch into a Giant powerhouse. The new American Football League was formed, and the scrappy bunch of upstarts were giving the NFL a run for its money and its fans.[11]

So in 1958, just as Middletown's Run and Shoot basketball team was garnering national attention, and professional football was bringing the gridiron sport into the hearts and minds of American spectators everywhere, Tiger Ellison was facing the worst football season in the history of Middletown High School. Each Sunday afternoon he would bring his

---

[11] Michael MacCambridge, *America's Game* (New York: Random House, 2004)

starters out to the house to go over the film of Friday's game so he could give them one-on-one attention to improve their assignments. But at midseason, they had posted no victories, four defeats, and one scoreless tie.

The Boosters' Club, which met on Mondays at the Manchester Hotel to go over the previous Friday's game, was always packed to the gills with fans eager to hear Tiger's intensive oratorical skills applied to the game film of the past week. He was always able to show them an informed analysis of game highlights, and where plays had broken down, and how they would be correcting for the upcoming game. But lately the mood at the Manchester had turned growly, the film showed more breakdowns than breakthroughs, and there were plenty of "downs" to go around. The team was down four losses and one tie at midseason. The boys were down because they knew they were letting the coach down. The coach knew he was letting the boys down. The town was down on both coach and players, and the depth of the downside was daunting.

Tiger spent extra time analyzing those five miserable games, telling himself that a great fall requires great energy to get up, that all the force which was failing to produce a winner would require great creative counterforce to rebound to new heights. He had a couple of talented sophomores sitting on the varsity bench who could have made the difference he was looking for, but through the years, he had tried very hard to showcase his seniors because he wanted to get as many as possible into college on scholarship. His five-ounce walnut-sized thinking brain was exhausted from analyzing that film and seeing milliseconds of bad timing, and unspirited sparkplugs that fired sluggishly, and muscles that failed to bunch for a burst of power.

I had looked at the problem so long that all my energy was caving in on it. That's sort of like seeing a beautiful woman with a small wart on her face; if all you focus on is that wart, pretty soon she's a big wart with a tiny little woman hiding behind it, if you know what I mean. I needed to look away from the problem, "Look where it ain't!" as my mom used to say, get a fresh perspective on things.

I told myself to forget the T-formation, just look at the field. My quarterback was not particularly fast, but he could scramble, and if I spread the field I would spread the defenders, and maybe he could get the ball to a receiver. I had called the league office to verify that my center could be an eligible receiver if he lined up at the end of the line. Just because he was called "Center" didn't actually mean he had to be in the center of the pack. That would give the quarterback one more guy to throw to. I started with those little ideas, but I had a lot more work to do.

So after the boys left the house that Sunday afternoon, I told Elsie I was going to go out for a ride just to clear my head and figure out the rest of this "spread 'em out across the field" idea. Mother Nature had provided a crisp autumn afternoon that day, full of vivid pictures of her own great field that reminded a man that God's handiwork was a far cry better than anything man could make. I stopped the car alongside a sandlot near the stadium on the south side of town, and watched an exuberant bunch of grade-schoolers tossing the football around and having a grand old time, playing a loosely structured, spontaneous, energetic little game called aerial.

The quarterback was a slender, willowy young man with a rubbery arm. He would scramble around big eyed and expectant as he studied his receivers cutting downfield right or left or deep or short, all depending on how the defenders were covering them. These youngsters were simply doing what comes naturally, letting the defense determine their pass cuts.

> He go right, I go left!
> He go left, I go right!
> He come here, I go there!
> He go there, I stay here!

These lads were thinking on the run! And they were having great fun doing it!

Tiger Ellison drove back home with a clear vivid picture of highly energized young boys having fun playing football. There were no set patterns here, no grind-it-out for three yards through a mass of humanity on the other side of the ball. They were simply "Looking where the defender ain't!" and making their cuts accordingly.

Now, Tiger was never a man to give up sleep over a problem. He knew a fellow needed a good night's sleep to wake up refreshed and ready to bound into the day with a clear mind.

But that night after about three hours of sleep, the ornery rascal called my subconscious mind woke me up with a "BOOM! Hey, bub, get up! Do I have some pictures for YOU!" The little rascal had been busy down under the surface while I slept, and by the time I woke up there was so much adrenalin pumping into my bloodstream that my heart was racing as pictures of a new concept flooded into my brain! I threw on some sweats, raced by my daughters' blackboard in the breezeway to pick up chalk, and bounded to the basement. I did about twenty-five overhand chin-ups, shook out my arms and pulled twenty underhanded ones, just to settle down a bit.

Then I took the chalk and drew six Jerry Lucas-type circles on the concrete floor, three at the line where I would start the offensive positions, three deep destination zones for running cuts and passing the football. The first circle I spread seventeen yards out to the left of the ball, and called it "Heaven," because that was where I would stretch most of my line and the left halfback, and that would play some glorious and inspired havoc with the defenders. The circle seventeen yards far to the right I called "Hell" and put the right halfback and fullback, lined up a yard and a half behind the line of scrimmage. That left my center at the end of the line in the middle circle, which I called "Boston." Personally, I had never quite figured out where Boston was in relation to Heaven and Hell, but my center would be eligible to receive from Boston.

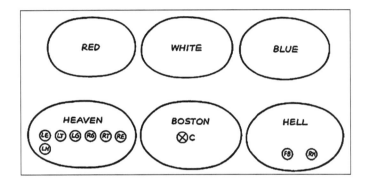

The three deep passing zones I called "Red, White and Blue," because that had a patriotic ring to it, and patriotism was one of a youth's greatest motivating forces. And if nothing else, my players needed to be motivated. Besides, it gave us a chance to describe plays in a way that was a lot of fun, like "Hotfoot it from Heaven and make a beeline for Boston," or "Spring forth from Hell into the deep Blue yonder!"

You would have to understand what a radical departure this was for me! I had always been a possession football coach who avoided calling any more pass plays than necessary, since three things can happen when you pass, and I hated two of them. Like every conventional coach, I was always focused on the three things that mattered most on each play: down, distance, and position on the field. But what this crazy offense was saying was, "To hell with that! Let's go for it on every play! Let's throw passes at will, put the football on display, give the fans something to cheer about, and have fun doing it!"

With the creative juices flowing, Tiger spent the rest of the night chalking out Xs and Os and arrows on the concrete floor, transferring them to a notebook and giving birth to the most widespread offense ever known to mankind. By morning he had a new playbook, all plays within the rules of the game, but all with the spirit and energy of aerial! This would be fun football as opposed to the meat-grinder variety that had not worked for the first half of the season. He needed to purge his football camp of the graveyard seriousness that had crept into every player and every coach in the previous five miserable weeks. He needed to use humor as a tonic for rock bottom morale. He didn't know whether they would win a single game with this new offense, but by God, it would be spirited!

He thought about calling it "The Lonesome Cowboy," since he had his quarterback lined up about eleven yards behind his center in Boston, all by his lonesome without a friendly jersey in sight to protect him. He thought most defenses would see this as an easy opportunity to pick off the lone gunman, and would rush in where angels fear to tread, leaving five eligible receivers to be defended by only the few poor fools remaining. It would be impossible for the defenders to anticipate what the offense was going to do on each play, since the offense was taking its cue from where the defenders lined up, and their cuts were determined by where the defender headed after the snap of the ball. And even though there were a dozen plays in the new playbook, with tradeoffs that could be made at the line, the quarterback did not have to worry because he knew he would always have one of his eligible receivers in each zone of Heaven, Hell, and the Red, White, and Blue. When a scramble was on, he would forget about going to Heaven, look for a friendly jersey in Boston, and he could still go to Hell.

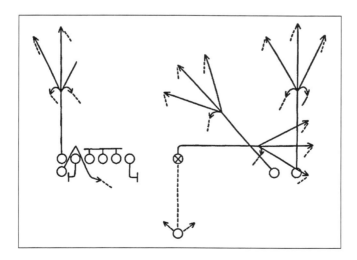

When Tiger got to the locker room on Monday afternoon, he had more energy than he ever dreamed possible after three short hours of sleep. He outlined the basics of the new offensive philosophy on the board, threw down the chalk and turned to his players and said, "I'm thinking about calling it the 'Lonesome Cowboy,' boys, what do you think?" His energy must have been contagious because his boys were on the edge of their seats or already pacing the floor, ready to get to the practice field and try the crazy thing. Every player in the place had a grin a mile wide on his formerly frustrated face. They gave a big cheer! His line coach Stan Lewis, however, had the grimace of a bad gas pain on his face, and said, "You'd better call it the 'Lonesome Polecat,' Tiger, because this skunk stinks!"

Thus was born the Lonesome Polecat offense, which brought the 1958 season back into the winning column and the fans back into the stands on Friday nights, to see the most wide-open aerial display of the pigskin ever witnessed by high school fans anywhere. During practice that first week, Tiger noticed a palpable surge in the energy level of his players, as everybody on the team had to think and make decisions, based on the defender in his path. And that individual energy poured into a spirit on the team that rivaled their predecessors of a decade earlier. They were pumped as they prepared to showcase the Lonesome Polecat that Friday night.

Undefeated Dayton Roosevelt came into Middletown's Barnitz Stadium that Friday, coached by former Detroit Lion fullback Ray Pelfrey. He had been a tough player and was a tough, competitive coach. But based on his scouting reports about the Middies' problems that season, Coach Pelfrey anticipated that his starters would be warming the bench by the middle of the second half. Out of respect for Tiger, he would not run the score up on him or risk possible injury to those young men who were outweighed by the Dayton players thirty pounds to the man.

The Middies received the opening kickoff and ran the ball back to midfield. Then without a huddle, they went into an offensive formation that looked strangely more like a punt formation than the first play from the line of scrimmage at midfield. The defenders were confused, but dutifully stretched out man-to-man across the field. The quarterback signaled the play with a baseball hand signal, and when the center was ready, he long-snapped the ball from Boston. Roy Lucas, at right end in Heaven, noticed his defender staying right with him, so he thought "He stay, I go!" and lit out for the big Red zone. He caught the pass and ran for the easiest fifty-yard touchdown play this team had ever made.

Because the defense was so spread out, they found that even the quarterback who had no natural running ability could ramble through the porous line on short yardage situations. Their place kicker had been injured in a previous game, so they decided they could just use the Lonesome Polecat to make two-point conversions after scoring. At halftime, Tiger found his boys' energy so high that he let his co-captain Jan Knepshield do the pep talking in the locker room. He was not about to interfere with that newly found spirit and the unbridled enthusiasm this team had just discovered for itself.

In the second half, Coach Pelfrey made a modification to the defense to rush the quarterback with a six-man enemy force, leaving five receivers open to more mischief because Polecat theory stated that all rushers automatically eliminated themselves from the play. By the fourth quarter, it was Middletown's starters who were sent to warm the bench. They won that game 24-14, giving up two touchdowns late in the game because they had not spent a lick of time on defense that week in practice.

At the final gun, my men were so excited you would have thought we had won the State Championship! I saw big ol' Ray Pelfrey charging across the field at me like a berserk bull hell-bent for election. I didn't know whether to run or start to pray! Then WHACK! He hit me on top of this old baldhead and said, "What in blazes was THAT you just threw at us tonight?" I said, "Ray, we call that the Lonesome Polecat. Somebody said it stinks and it couldn't be done, but we did it! I think it's so fine I may have to call it Sir Lonesome Polecat!"

That Sunday when the boys came out to the house to study the game film, my quarterback took me aside and told me he had spent the previous Sunday night on the banks of the Miami River contemplating suicide. I thanked him for having the strength of character not to do that, and said, "You can never outguess the Big Man's plan for you, son. Problems are given to us for a reason, to be solved. The greater the challenge, the more we must reach into our God-given talents and muster the will to break through. And just think of what you would have missed!" It shook me up to think of how much had been riding on the bold move we had just made.

The Lonesome Polecat won every game for the rest of the season. It saved the head coach and taught him a new philosophy for playing American football. The fans loved the aerial display and once again began filling the stadium on Friday nights. And most importantly to Tiger, his players believed in themselves again. Salvation, as it turned out, had only been one game away.

Tiger had spent three years studying the T-formation, adapting a combination of Sid Gilman's version, the Chicago Bears', and Southern Cal's, before bringing his version to the Middletown Middies. The Lonesome Polecat had been the product of one desperate season. He knew that this wily little Polecat would lose its element of surprise and was not a complete offense, but it had taught him some things. First, if the coach only has a guy who can throw the football and four guys who can catch it, the team can score touchdowns with average material at the other positions. Second, he learned that passing on the run could be done just as accurately and as far as passing from a set position. These two lessons would modify his offensive designs as he went into the off-season to begin planning for the next year.

The third lesson was more philosophical. When each player had to engage his mind, assess the defender's actions, and make decisions on the spot, his energy and attention elevated and his execution improved dramatically. This fit so well with Tiger's personal philosophy for coaching and teaching: engage the thinking mind, tie in the subconscious with a moving picture, get the adrenalin pumping into the bloodstream for unleashed energy, and the motions that follow will be the best they can be. That would build confidence and courage, on the field and in the game of life. For Tiger, this seemed like an American ideal! The educational value of football would take on a whole new meaning, and possession football would have to give way to this new energy and philosophy.

In the spring of 1959, as Tiger continued to develop new ideas for his offense, he was selected by the Freedom's Foundation of Valley Forge to be among the first group of educators across the country to receive the newly struck Valley Forge Classroom Teachers Gold Medal, "for exceptional work in teaching a better understanding of the American way of life." School Board President Joe Woodruff said at the time, "Tiger Ellison, through his life, work, leadership, and personal example, has gone far beyond his duties as a teacher in our schools, to inspire young people to a better appreciation of freedom's fundamentals, regardless of race, creed, color, or social status. We are grateful to have such a great American teaching our young people." Of all the honors and awards that Tiger had accumulated through his forty-eight years, this particular one captured the essence of what made his life's work so enjoyable for him. He had that medal mounted into a small frame, and he hung it inconspicuously on the wall in his living room for the rest of his life. The coach was, after all, first and foremost a teacher.

10

OPERATION RUN AND SHOOT: THE BOY GROWS UP

The Lonesome Polecat offense had produced such skillful motion on the field and enthusiastic emotion in the stands that the Middletown sportswriters and fans went hog wild for wide-open football, proving that fans love seeing the pigskin on display. There was no need for them to wait for Monday's Boosters' Club at the Manchester Hotel to see the football play itself out in the slow motion of the film review. They learned they could turn off their television sets on Friday night, pay their money to go to the stadium, and watch the whole exciting aerial display of fluid football in real time, a show so spectacular that it rivaled anything on TV.

But while the Lonesome Polecat was a boy born of the desperate need and creative mind of the coach, that boy was about to mature into the Run and Shoot offense that would father the most productive and skillful offensive schemes ever known in the history of the game. While the Run and Shoot would never forget its Polecat roots in reading defenses to determine play calls and route conversions after the snap, it would leave behind its childlike antics in favor of a more sophisticated scheme that would produce one touchdown every ten plays, and average five touchdowns per game, for the next four years at Middletown High School.

Tiger called his new offense Run and Shoot, borrowing the term from Coach Walker's fast and fluid basketball philosophy, where the players would run anywhere they needed to get open and score. Run and Shoot football was designed to make every run look like a pass, and every pass look like a run, with the whole field considered offensive territory. He designed each play from a single formation, putting his center back into the middle of the pack, since he had learned in half a season with the Lonesome Polecat that spreading the field made it unnecessary to have his center doubling as an eligible receiver. The formation was perfectly symmetrical, with a double-slot and the two ends split seventeen yards to each side of the tackles. The linesmen split at two-foot intervals, all of which opened up room for the run and forced the defenders out of their nine-man front. Since the four receivers always lined up this way on every play, the defense had to keep three men back to protect against the possibility of a long pass.

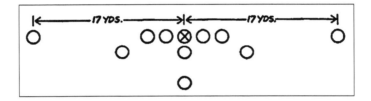

Tiger was the first coach to number each of the defenders on the front side and the back side, with plays designed and called based on setup and movement of one specific opponent. All the offensive plays began with a man in motion, then developed as they watched the defensive reaction.

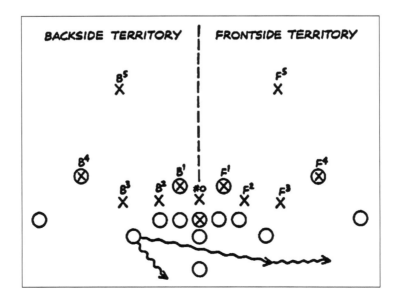

From the opening whistle to the final gun, the Run and Shoot offense had the potential to score on every play, except for the occasional punt. We only averaged 1.2 punts per contest in those four years because we considered any place on the field to be offensive territory.

During our possession football days, we had to arrive at the opponent's forty before we considered ourselves in scoring position. We had reasoned that, since the offense knew exactly what route it would take and where it would strike after the play was called in the huddle, the defense would need a split second to react to the movement and another second or so to determine the point of attack. Plus if they had done their scouting correctly, they could anticipate which play we were likely to call in any given situation of down, distance, and field position. Plays were *preprogrammed* so that defenses could prepare on paper and in practice to shut us down at game time.

But with the Run and Shoot, we *reprogrammed* our plays based on what the defense was giving us, eliminating the predictability and frustrating the defenders no end. They could no longer just play like a herd of husky buffaloes stomping the hell out of us because this offense was slippery at movement and ball handling. We made every pass look like a run and every run look like a pass. All the linemen used the same kind of block whether the play was a run or a pass. There was no crossfield blocking to tip off a run because our ends were split out too far to make it across to the far side. Instead, they always went downfield toward the defending halfback on their side, either to catch a pass, to stalk the deep defender before throwing a block into his lap, or to lure him away from a running play on the other side. The beauty of it was that the defender was clueless until he saw the pigskin being delivered across the line of scrimmage either by land or by loft. That neutralized monster defenses and gang tackling, and ended up reducing injuries as well.

This was fun football! No more a war of attrition, where each team hauled forth the heavy armor and threw a siege on the opposing camp to wear them away. This was a war of movement, finesse, and graceful ball-handling skill!

Now, fun football is a relative term. Tiger was still tough on his players, demanding every ounce of their energy and every spark of their spirit on the practice field and on game night. If they practiced lazy, they would play sloppy. If they came to play just good enough, they would find the coach pushing them relentlessly to give more and stretch out those personally defined limits. Some players would break down and quit because they did not like being goaded into performing at that level. Some would break out in anger and let their seething anger motivate them. Most would break through into a higher level of performance than they knew they had in them, and discover the confidence that comes from striving to become the best one can be.

Tiger knew that the new offense was a "Thinking Man's Offense," requiring more mental toughness, agility, discipline, and precision teamwork, than the mere brute force, strength, and bulk of conventional football. If the Run and Shoot were to live up to the potential envisioned in the mind of the coach, his boys would need to elevate their skill and confidence to perform and to make good decisions. Tiger's enthusiasm for his new offense came not only from the fact that it would make the skill positions on the team more productive, but also from its educational value in building the confidence and character of his players.

During the year of the Polecat, Tiger had left some talented sophomores on the bench to showcase his seniors. But by the summer of 1959, as the summer dog days approached and he had settled on five series of plays which would become the core of his Run and Shoot, he needed to tap his best players, in order to give the new offense a chance to prove itself. Quarterback Bill Triick spent the summer before his junior year practicing the drills that would make the rhythm and mobility of passing on the run second nature to him. He spent several hours of every afternoon zinging the football into a stationary target, from a step sequence to the left or to the right. Then whenever possible he would get a group of his teammates together to play aerial, running and shooting with no predefined play calls and no coach hovering over them. They found this kind of conditioning not only useful for developing the mobility and instincts for an aerial attack, but also a lot more fun than lifting weights and digging ditches all summer to prepare for the fall grind of conventional football. And every day as his skills improved, Bill Triick became noticeably more confident in his ability to lead an offense.

The team had two weeks in August to learn the plays, but many had already developed the instincts for passing on the run and reading defenses. They used the first game of the season to master the complexities of the two split ends, the flankered halfbacks in the slots, and the man-in-motion maneuver, but for the rest of the season they never looked back, scoring an average of thirty-four points per game for a tremendous, freewheeling, fan-pleasing, winning year. Establishing himself as the best quarterback in the Greater Ohio League as a junior, Bill Triick either broke or tied every quarterback record in the book except one.

In their senior year, the team elected Triick, along with his speedy receiver Jim Gillis, to lead them on the field as co-captains. In this second year of the Run and Shoot, Bill would ask Tiger before each game which series they should use to start the game. At midseason, Tiger began turning the question back to him, and went with the recommendations. In the fourth quarter of one of those games, the Middies were behind on fourth down, with four yards to go, precious seconds left on the clock, and no timeouts remaining. The quarterback looked to the sidelines to see if the punter was coming in, but there was no movement in that direction. So he looked to the coach for a play call, but there was no movement in that direction either, just the stoic look of a coach looking back at him. He and Gillis made the decision in the huddle to send their most talented and trusted receiver, Billy Crowe, out on a long downfield pass route that wasn't even in the playbook. They knew Crowe was the guy in pressure situations they could count on the most to outmaneuver the defenders and make the winning score. Triick's pass connected, and they won, all with a confidence that none would have exhibited just a few years earlier.

Bill Triick was selected as All State quarterback that year, and would earn an appointment to the United States Military Academy at West Point in the spring, an appointment based not only on scholastic achievement, but also on physical preparedness and leadership ability. He would go on to serve his country as an Army officer, and then become a leader in business and his community in the years ahead. He was a real winner.

Jim Gillis was a real winner with a different story. He was motivated by a seething anger deeply embedded in his soul from a very early age. He had been born with what today would be recognized as a learning disability. But in those days there were no special education programs geared to special needs, and the kids were simply relegated to the Thomas A. Edison School, which was affectionately known in the neighborhood as "the Dumb School." Not much was taught at the Dumb School because the kids were considered too slow and incapable of learning academic subjects. For the few whose parents wanted them mainstreamed into Middletown High School to continue their education, no special tutoring or counseling was offered to help them adjust or to build an academic foundation and study habits. The expectations about kids from the Dumb School most often became a self-fulfilling prophecy.

Jim Gillis felt the frustration and fury that seemed to be the unshakeable stigma of the Dumb School. He had to dig deep into his very young soul to find the strength to overcome the low expectations others had of him. He had to work overtime just to get to the starting line of the rest of the kids in the race. But dig deep he did, and the deep-seated anger and sense of injustice that he felt for those around him who expected him to fail only fanned his own incredible will to win. He played football as part of expressing that self-determined spirit to prove them all wrong.

His anger was particularly directed at Coach Tiger Ellison. He knew Tiger thought he was too dumb to spell "Cat." The coach rode him relentlessly in practice, pushing him to perform better. He suspected the man was a racist at heart. Jim's anger would wake him up at all hours of the night, and with teeth and fists clenched, he vowed he would prove the coach and all the rest of them wrong.

He played spectacular football at Middletown High as a Run and Shoot receiver and team leader. With the help of Choppy and Laverne Saunders, he was able to survive the academic challenges of high school studies that had been badly crippled by years at the Dumb School. Choppy had a friend who was athletic director at Tennessee State, and Jim earned a football scholarship. It would take him five years to graduate, but he made it. He went on to become one of the best assistant coaches and Special Education teachers the Middletown School System ever had.

Anger can be a huge motivator when it is directed toward cultivating self-determination and the personal will to win against any injustice. It would take Jim Gillis well into the reflective stage of his retirement years to realize that the anger that had pushed him to excel against incredible odds had been displaced by his deep spiritual commitment to be a real winner. No one else needed to tell him how good he was. He had found the strength within himself to build an incredibly fulfilling life, helping countless others with similar problems along the way. Excellence was its own reward, and Jim found the peace that comes with perseverance and personal performance.

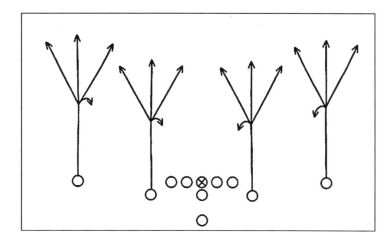

During those first two years of Run and Shoot football at Middletown High School, much to the coach's amazement, many opponents refused to come out of their nine-man fronts or spread their deep defenders to cover the split ends. That was great for the Tiger team because it would always result in the quarterback flipping an easy automatic pass to the sidelines. Because of the angles, the defender would have to travel the long side of a triangle to try to break up the automatic pass, and in four years not one of those passes was ever intercepted. If the defense loaded up on one side, a quick flip to the back side would punish the opponent. If they tried to double cover both ends, they left only a six-man front facing off with a nine-man offensive unit with huge running potential. Any rush would result in a scramble that essentially took the linemen out of the play.

But the biggest headache of all was created for the secondary defender. He could not anticipate run or pass because this crazy ball club would pass anywhere on the field on any down. He could not read "pass" when the ends came downfield or the quarterback set up in the pocket because the ends *always* came downfield and the quarterback *never* set up in a pocket, since he always passed on the run. He could not read "run" from crossfield blocking because the ends and tackles never blocked across the field. But the most confounding thing was that he never seemed able to anticipate where the receiver was going, left or right, short or long because he always seemed to go the opposite way. And every millisecond of indecision by the defender worked to the advantage of this mobile offense.

The Run and Shoot was clearly a radical departure from conventional "three yards and a cloud of dust" football, in philosophy and formation and the resulting playbook. It frustrated defenses and required a complete corresponding rethink of defensive coaching. The variations and possibilities seemed limitless to Tiger as he refined his thinking about this new offense, but in spite of the temptation to create a profusion of new plays, he disciplined himself to hone in on the number of plays his boys could practice in one day. He settled on five series of plays so his team could go through the entire repertoire every day in practice, a requirement he thought would be necessary for any offense that features the ball on display.

Savvy was quickly becoming Tiger's new favorite S-word, as he had seen what the requirement to think and interpret and make on-the-spot decisions had done for the spirit of his teams. This was not simply "Get there the fustest with the mostest!" and outpower the opponent. Run and Shoot was tactical, not strategically preprogrammed. It threw everybody into motion and placed a premium on skillful movement and ball handling. And Tiger learned that the fans would pay to see such a skillful performance. The fans *loved* it and packed the stadium on game nights. Motion begat emotion, which led to *commotion* in the stands!

He quite frankly didn't know how he would defend against this offense, but since his was the first team to use it, he wouldn't need to worry about running into it from the other side for a few years. It would not take long to discover that the moment would come sooner rather than later. The clinics that Tiger attended every year to learn from other coaches were beginning to generate a huge interest in the wide-open brand of football being showcased at Middletown High School. Film that he sent off to colleges to help his players get those coveted scholarships would more often than not result in coaches asking to learn more about the system Tiger was using. He soon found himself conducting more clinics than he was attending, which he was happy to do because he thought Run and Shoot had great potential at all levels of the game. Innovative coaches always shared new offensive strategies in the spirit of making American football and its coaches and players better each year.

The questions that came in from coaches around the country and at clinics usually started with a "Yeah, but . . ." The favorite one, from possession coaches who had not been immersed in the new philosophy as Tiger had for two years, was always, "Yeah, but, you had an exceptionally talented passer in All State quarterback Bill Triick. If I knew I'd have a quarterback like that every year, I might try this Run and Shoot." What Tiger knew was that Bill Triick and the next two starting quarterbacks that would follow him in that four-year period had all come to Tiger rated as average passers by their junior high coaches. But they all had the self-discipline and work ethic and smarts to learn the mobility and ball handling required by this offense. Each one drove his own performance from average to exceptional, and all were selected as All State quarterbacks their senior year. The Run and Shoot offense made them more productive, and they all were in demand from big schools recruiting them for football scholarships.

So in 1961, the third season for the Run and Shoot, when John McCluskey was in line to become starting quarterback for Middletown, he represented a major question for all the skeptics on several dimensions. John had been the backup for Bill Triick for two years and had not seen a lot of action in those games. Even the sportswriters of the *Middletown Journal* expressed skepticism about whether any young man could fill the footsteps of Triick's record-breaking performance with this new offense.

John's neighborhood buddies teased him no end about the likelihood of a black quarterback starting for Middletown High School anytime soon. The only one who would have no part of that was Jim Gillis, who for two years as an upperclassman had constantly encouraged John to stay positive, ignore the skeptics, and go for his goal. Ohio's predominantly white schools in the early '60s didn't have black starting quarterbacks, since the conventional wisdom of the day was that blacks were not smart enough to play quarterback, and teammates would not respond to their leadership. And Run and Shoot obviously required more thinking and on-field leadership than conventional football.

John had watched two-a-day practices at Barnitz Stadium ever since he had been a little boy, and while tales of Tiger's rigor and the booming baritone of the coach himself may have put the fear of the Lord in him while he was younger, he knew in his mind he was smart, prepared, and determined enough to assume the helm for the Run and Shoot. John McCluskey, as a matter of fact, was a serious-minded, brilliant young man. Not only was he quietly intense, intelligent, and hardworking, but he also had a rich sense of humor and the positive attitude to keep the skeptics at bay. As a student, he had never missed making the honor roll, and he was tapped for the National Honor Society in his junior year. He got along so well with his classmates that they elected him to be vice president of the senior class. His teammates selected him as the co-captain of the football team. And Tiger Ellison tapped him for the starting quarterback position as a senior.

In the sultry heat of August in 1961, Tiger had scheduled a practice scrimmage with Cincinnati Purcell. The Catholic schools in Cincinnati played some tough football in those days, and the Middletown players were well aware of it. John watched as the big yellow school bus pulled up to Barnitz Stadium, and what seemed like an endless number of huge, intimidating, high-tonnage animals-on-the-hoof emerged to play football. Cerebral as he was, John was not prepared to feel his butterflies start to flutter and flap in anticipation of running and shooting into that mass of humanity known as Cincinnati Purcell.

The Middies performed poorly, and at halftime Tiger pulled his quarterback aside. John braced himself for the Tiger rage he had heard so often as a kid watching two-a-days. But instead, Tiger looked at him intently, eyeball-to-eyeball, and calmly began:

John, you are a "Thinking Man's Quarterback" and I respect you for that. You have all the knowledge, skill, and preparation you need to lead this team, and your teammates want to see that in you. If you have no confidence in yourself, your teammates will read that in your eyes, and they will have no confidence in you either. Your opponents will see it instantly, and take *every* advantage of it they can, in the game of football and in the game of life.

I am seeing something in your eyes, and it looks to me like its name is Fear. It may not *be* Fear, but your eyes are telegraphing Fear. You only need Fear when you have absolutely no idea what you are doing or how to do it. You know perfectly well what you want to do out there and how to get it done. But Fear is paralyzing your ability and sapping your energy. Fear is getting in your way, blocking and tackling your knowledge and instincts.

Fear is signaling indecision to your teammates and opportunity to your opponents.

Leadership is not just what's in your mind, John, it's also what's in your heart and soul. You must feel the Faith in your heart that you can lead this team. When you feel Faith in your heart, it will show in your eyes, and others will see it there. Your teammates want to see confidence in your eyes, and they will respond in kind and get the job done. Faith will outperform Fear every time and shut it down. I want to see your confidence and intensity bursting from your heart and blazing in those eyes of yours! Now go out there and lead this team with conviction!

John McCluskey went on to lead his team to a nine-and-one season, breaking all the records set the year before. He became Ohio's first black All State quarterback, and in the spring was aggressively recruited by several Big Ten schools. He was all set to attend Northwestern University and play football for Ara Parseghian on a full scholarship, when an alumnus of Harvard came to Middletown to talk to Tiger about this scholastically gifted young black leader.

John, Ara wants you at Northwestern and Woody wants you at Ohio State. You could have your college education paid for completely and play great, competitive football. Harvard wants you to play football for them, but they are more interested in your scholastic achievement. Harvard doesn't offer fully paid athletic scholarships, but they offer an education and opportunity like no other. You would have to work some jobs and take out some student loans to go to Harvard.

You need to think about that, and decide whether you want to take on the risk of the academic challenge and financial debt in order to achieve an outstanding opportunity for life. Look into your head and look into your heart, and decide what you want to do. I will support your decision either way.

With the support of his parents as well, John decided he had the confidence and positive determination to take his chances at Harvard, and he never looked back. He not only excelled academically, but he started as varsity quarterback for the Harvard football team both his junior and senior year. Overheard in the pubs of Boston's working class Irish neighborhoods were fans who were mighty proud, when they read the headline of the *Boston Globe* Sports Section that one of their own Irish laddies named McCluskey would be leading the football team of this Ivy

League bastion of intellectualism. They drank their beer and bought their tickets to celebrate the season opener between McCluskey's Harvard and the University of Massachusetts. Perhaps they were surprised by his first appearance on the field, but they could not have been disappointed in the performance of Harvard's first black starting quarterback, the first in the Ivy League. John McCluskey had become a leader on many dimensions, Irish name or not, football skeptics or not.

After Harvard, John went on to earn his postgraduate degree from Stanford and become adjunct professor of English and dean of African American Studies at Indiana University, teaching and mentoring many a young person to reach for the best they had in them, demanding with telegraphed intensity that they commit mind, body, and soul to their worthy goals.

Lingering skeptics of the Run and Shoot remained, waiting to see if Tiger could get lucky enough to find a dazzling quarterback for the third time in a row. This time it was Paul Walker, Jr., son of the school's championship basketball coach, who would step up to lead Run and Shoot football at Middletown High.

As a youngster, Paul had excelled at the wide-open philosophy on the hard court, and with some practice drills and coaching, he became a natural at running and shooting on the gridiron. After he had turned in a nine-and-one season, high school and college coaches around the country began to set their skepticism aside and realize that Run and Shoot football could indeed make average teams good, good teams great, and *every* team more productive on the scoreboard. Three different quarterbacks in four years, with thirty-eight victories and only seven losses, had captured the attention of many a coach and legitimized the Run and Shoot as a fast, powerful, and deceptive scheme that could overwhelm modern defenses, which in recent years had threatened to stalemate other football offenses. The proof was in the performance. Average kids had become exceptionally productive in the exciting art of passing, catching, running, and dodging defenders, the very skills that were about to make wide-open football the darling of America's sports spectators in the years ahead, from neighborhood little league teams all the way to the NFL.

11

RUN AND SHOOT GOES TO COLLEGE

> For four years our new offense had featured wide-open running as well as passing in about equal amounts, and it proved to be absolutely sensational. Nobody could stop it. We couldn't even stop it ourselves. One night we scored 98 points against Portsmouth, Ohio, one of our longtime rivals. We didn't intend to humiliate those fine people that way. But we couldn't turn the crazy thing off. When the embarrassing fiasco was over, our third-string quarterback was the top scorer in the Greater Ohio League. Amazing!

After the New Year in 1963, Tiger began to be inundated with phone calls and letters from high school and college coaches from across the country, asking him to send them information, or come and speak to their players and coaches, or conduct clinics about the Run and Shoot offense. In the days before home computers and emails and video recorders, he bought himself a used Royal typewriter and a mimeograph machine, along with a manual gadget for copying and splicing 8-millimeter film, all just to keep up with the demand.

The excitement generated by the new offense may have been just a curiosity for some, but for Tiger, the growing interest was exhilarating. At that time perhaps he alone knew that its potential for making coaches and players more productive, and spectators more intrigued and enthusiastic about America's greatest fighting game, had barely been tapped. He energetically responded to every request he could, knowing full well that the way to exploit its potential was to get other coaches understanding the philosophy and running with the possibilities. But with a full teaching and coaching load during the school year, he was challenged to keep up with the overwhelming demand.

Then one day, just as the correspondence backlog was piling up, as if by some act of fate, a call came in from an editor at Parker Publishing Company in New York. The man introduced himself as the head of their Sports Publishing Division, and indicated that their surveys from coaches in their book club were showing an increasing interest in this wide-open offensive scheme called Run and Shoot. He asked Tiger if he would write a book about it.

For Tiger this seemed a perfect solution to spreading the gospel according to Run and Shoot. With his conviction about its potential to elevate the game, and with a modicum of confidence that he could tell a story in writing just as well as he could on the speaking circuit, Tiger agreed to write a book on *Run and Shoot Football: Offense of the Future*. He had lots of material from the clinics he had conducted, and all he needed was that chunk of time offered by two months off in the summer to dedicate to the draft of a manuscript.

At age fifty-two, Tiger considered that perhaps destiny was moving him in the direction of coaching the younger coaches and making his contribution to the game in that way. He had already earned his master's degree in English in the previous summers, and he began to think about writing as a way to give back to the profession that had made his life work so much fun. It would be a labor of love.

Then another call came in, this one at midnight on a Friday in late January. It was Woody Hayes.

A man ought to be in bed asleep at midnight, which is exactly where I was. But the confounded phone just kept ringing like there was no tomorrow, so I finally jumped out of bed, shook my head a couple of times, and grabbed the phone from the wall in the kitchen. Woody said, "Did I wake you, Tiger?" I said, "Oh, hell, Woody, that's okay. I had to get up anyway to answer the darned phone!" I would learn in the years ahead that midnight was just the middle of the working day for Woody!

"Tiger, I've asked you twice since taking this job at Ohio State a dozen years ago to come up here and coach with me, but you always said Middletown was the greatest city in the country for bringing up your little girls, and you loved coaching and teaching those high school kids more than anything. So my first question is, how many more little girls do you have at home?"

I told him my baby Carolyn was a freshman at Miami just down the road in Oxford, the last of the litter to leave home. So he said, "Well, you probably don't know this yet, but Bo Schembechler is leaving my staff to take the head coaching job at Miami, and I need another strong man who can put up with my temperament but also help me get this team back into championship form again. Now, damn it, Tiger, don't you say no until we can talk about it. Will you come up here and talk to me, man?"

I told him I'd come up in the morning. So before dawn, I jumped into the Buick and drove to his office in Columbus, and he was still there. I don't know when the man slept!

Columbus, Ohio, unlike Cleveland and Cincinnati, never had a professional sports team of its own. But it really didn't need one because all the local fans and loyal alumni of this big university town put all their fanaticism and love of the sport behind Buckeye football. Businesses in town would close down, and traffic patterns would be modified to flow only one way on game day, into the parking lot of the Horseshoe Stadium. These fans enthusiastically glorified the team and the coach when they had winners and a high national ranking, but became just as vocal and unhappy when their Buckeyes lost more than a few games.

The head coach's job at this powerhouse was a pressure cooker position, which was just the way Woody liked it. In the years preceding his arrival on the job, the program had seen a succession of six coaches in twelve years come and go. But Woody had secured his right to be there in the late fifties by bringing home two undisputed National Championships and Rose Bowl victories, and he was fast becoming a coaching legend. However, there was very little tolerance for mediocre seasons, and the losing season he had in 1959 helped him realize there would never be any such thing as automatic tenure for the head football coach of the Ohio State University, legendary or not.

One could also say that sometimes even in great victory, there can be defeat. As a result of those two great championships and the ensuing national media attention paid to the university's football program, some in the faculty and Alumni Club started expressing concern that football was besmirching the reputation of Ohio State as a fine academic institution. The logic seemed a little loopy because Buckeye football caused many a well-heeled alum to generously open the checkbook and proudly donate to the university's coffers. But politics in large academic institutions sometimes prevails over logic. So in 1961, after Woody had led his team through an undefeated season and had been invited to play in the Rose Bowl for another National Championship, the Faculty Council in its infinite wisdom voted to deny the team the opportunity.

Woody was stung by the decision because it was so unjust to his players who had worked so hard and earned the right to play for the big one. And even though in the following spring, the university overturned the fateful decision in perpetuity, the damage was done for the longer term. Ohio high school coaches no longer automatically fed their best players into Ohio's premier football program, and other Big Ten and Pac Eight schools could recruit at will in the state, pointing to the historical precedent as proof that OSU was de-emphasizing football.[12]

So Ohio State began losing some of its best high school talent to competitors. Many of those recruiters were quick to point out Woody's reputation for being a tough, hot-tempered coach to work for, and with changing social norms starting to creep into the younger generation of the early '60s, not every good high school player could handle his intense personal style. Those who played for him knew that his personal loyalty and earnest care for his players more than offset those demanding characteristics, but the program was not for everybody.

Woody was a stubborn, predictable, power-T-formation, possession football coach extraordinaire. There was very little innovation in his offense, and if he called forty pass plays in an entire season, that was about twice as many as usual for him. The most deceptive scheme he had was the elusive question of whether he would run his huge, powerful fullback off the left tackle or the right tackle. He admittedly had no instinct for coaching the passing game. And since he maintained a military-like control over every aspect of the game as the commanding officer of the team, Tiger Ellison could not imagine how his newly found love of wide-open football could possibly fit into a program under the direction of General Woody Hayes.

Tiger was well aware of Woody's temperament going back to their college days at Denison. But while he did not embrace some of his conduct with players and his antics with officials, he did understand and respect the man. Woody had an intensity and sincere passion for winning football games that Tiger shared and admired. During their college days, Woody had been a boxer and Tiger a wrestler, and therein lay a difference in approach that showed up in their coaching styles. The boxer would try to punch and pummel the living stuffings out of his opponent. The wrestler would use his power to finesse and outmaneuver the other guy. Ohio State football under Woody Hayes was a game of unrequited power and pummel and possession, not a game of graceful mobility and ball handling. Their discussion that day would be interesting.

---

[12] John Lombardo, *A Fire to Win: The Life and Times of Woody Hayes* (New York: Thomas Dunne Books, St. Martin's Press, 2005)

Woody greeted me like the old friend that he was, and we went over to the Student Union's Faculty Lounge to get a bite of breakfast. And just like he knew the questions I had on my mind, he said, "Tiger, you are rapidly becoming known as the passing-est coach in the country, and I guess I'm known as the non-passing-est coach that ever lived. But the pros, especially that upstart AFL, have been opening up the game for a few years, and now that's beginning to drift down to the college level. I don't have an instinct for coaching that kind of game, and I need your help on that front. I suppose I'll eventually need a full-time quarterback coach, but in the meantime I want you to work with my quarterbacks."

I said, "Woody, I'd be happy to help any coach and any quarterback develop his instincts for running and shooting the football. In fact, I'm going to write a book about that." That was not the sale Woody was trying to make, however. So the consummate salesman that he was moved on to a different tack. Military tactician at work!

"Tiger, I've coached some great players who came out of your program at Middletown—Rocko Joslin and Bobby Grimes, to mention just a couple—and I know how much respect those guys had for you. See, you didn't just demand the best of them on the field, you reached them in the heart and gave them purpose. They loved you.

"Remember our assistant coach Tommy Rogers at Denison? He was exactly what every young player needs on the coaching staff, a father figure who will give him guidance and teach him to succeed, academically and on the field and in his life. I want you to be my permanent freshman coach for as long as you want it, get those youngsters acclimated to college and their studies, get them ready to deal with tough ol' Woody. How is it you say that? 'Coach the kids, build the boys, mold the men.'

"You have the respect of every high school coach in this state. Hell, they even elected you to run their state coaches' association two different years and coach the Southern All Stars four times. I need your help in reaching those coaches and recruiting those top athletes so we can keep those boys in Ohio. We've had some challenges on that front lately.

"If you want to write a book, you don't want to target it just for the high school level and lower, I've heard you say that at your clinics. You need the college level of experience on your résumé to convince coaches to try your Run and Shoot at higher levels of the game. If we can introduce some of it at a powerhouse like Ohio State, you'll have yourself much greater credibility to affect the game for the long run."

Woody was indeed the consummate salesman. He had me on every point! It sounded like a perfect fit and an exciting opportunity! It would be great fun to coach the freshmen and help those young high school boys become mature college men. Woody even encouraged me to take the two months off in the summer to write my little epistle on Run and Shoot, something that by this time I was really looking forward to doing.

Tiger drove back to Middletown and by March, he and Elsie had found a home in Columbus to begin a new phase of their lives. Their youngest daughter Carolyn had the choice of staying at Miami or transferring, but the thought of going to a college that had as many matriculating students as her hometown had people was an exciting idea. She would become a Buckeye.

The coach who would take over the football program at Middletown was none other than Jack "Flash" Gordon, the Hamilton running back who in 1948 had denied Tiger his state championship on the last play of the last game of the season. He would talk to Tiger at least twice a week by phone so he could master all the finer points of Middletown's sensational offense, and the team continued to have great success. But at least once a month, Tiger could not help saying to him, "Jackie, I love ya, man. But I can never forgive you for taking away my state championship!" Coaches of every stripe just love to win!

Tiger began his new assignment as freshman and quarterback coach with the same positive intensity he put into everything else he did in his life. He and Woody had developed a great mutual respect for each other over more than thirty years of friendship and professional association. They understood each other's strengths and vulnerabilities, and knew just how far they could push each other in a test of wills that was well matched. Woody was confident Tiger would respect his role as head coach, but he also invited this innovative seasoned veteran to challenge his thinking about the offense. He was well aware that the game was changing at the college level, that the big schools were approaching parity in their talent pools, and that his brand of predictable smashmouth power football was running up against more potent defenses every year.

When Tiger arrived at his first coaches' meeting before the March spring practice sessions began, Woody tossed him the chalk and told him to give them a briefing on the philosophy and foundations of Run and Shoot. After an hour or so, he turned to the group and was greeted with enthusiastic energy coming back at him from all the coaches except one. Woody was standing there with his arms folded over his chest and a snarly bulldog expression engulfing his face. No sale, not this day! He moved over to the board and wrote "ROBUST" in big letters, and the rest of the spring was spent on the powerful pulverizing T-formation that was his signature offense. General Hayes would not move easily from his trusted battle plan, although Tiger and the other assistant coaches would continue to nudge him over the next five years.

When that first summer came around, and Tiger prepared to begin work on his manuscript, he discovered that Woody Hayes had no off-season. He simply could not help himself; he was a man obsessed with every aspect of the Ohio State football program. He would call two or three times a day, and pull Tiger away from home at least three or four times a week, to discuss player personnel, or game strategy for each upcoming rival, or academic schedules for players. He would ask Tiger to meet with faculty members, or take a speech for him, or meet with parents who were visiting campus to get the lay of the land. Sometimes he would just engage in philosophical conversation, observing changing social norms and reminiscing about the good old days when air was clean and sex was dirty, or he would commiserate on the growing student unrest about the Vietnam War. When Tiger would want to go home for dinner, Woody would become agitated, even accusing him of being some sort of oversexed animal because he liked spending time at home with his wife, a concept foreign to the head coach.

I knew Woody was sincere in his passion for Ohio State football, everything from winning games, to keeping his players academically grounded, to connecting with faculty and alumni. The only problem I had was finding that total immersion time I needed to organize and write my book in those so-called months off. The contract I had signed with Parker Publishing allowed three years to complete the project, but it was pretty clear that three years with Woody could come and go without a single page being written.

So I told him that the following summer, Elsie and I would be packing up the Royal typewriter and going to Florida to work on the manuscript. He laughed and said, "You better do that, Tige, and get yourself an unlisted phone number down there, or you'll never get the damned thing written! And it's a very important contribution to the game."

It was not hard at all to get mad at Woody, but it was impossible to *stay* mad at him. He knew himself pretty well. And he was loyal to the core to his players and coaches.

For the next few years, every spring the assistant coaches would bring up suggestions for a more balanced offense to the headman. And every spring Woody would listen silently with his trademark snarly jowl fixed firmly in place, then immediately gravitate back to his old pulverizing T. And every spring Tiger would work with the quarterbacks to build their agility and confidence in scrambling and throwing on the run. But every fall, Woody could not bring himself to call those pass plays in the arsenal because his instincts had been grooved on too many years of "three yards and a cloud of dust," grind-it-out success.

At one meeting Tiger good-naturedly said, "Yep, smashmouth football is the whole nine yards at OSU!" Woody blew up in one of his mega-ton rages, recognizing the implication that three yards three times doesn't move the chains. He picked up a nearby tape recorder and hurled it across the room at Tiger, who ducked adroitly as the device smashed to smithereens against the back wall. Years of Mississippi mud ball had taught him how to dodge incoming missiles a whole lot smaller than that thing. Woody roared, "What the hell kind of quarterback coach are you? You couldn't even *catch* the damned thing?"

With his freshmen team, Tiger was able to introduce all sorts of innovative offensive plays because the freshmen's main job was to run the opponent's offense against the varsity in preparation for the upcoming game. And many of those rival schools were moving rapidly toward more balanced and complex formations. Several schools in the Southeast Conference and Pac Eight were using the evolving I-formation with great success, and coaches all over the country were paying attention and attending clinics to learn new ways to incorporate the more complex and agile maneuvers into their game plans.

In 1965 Parker Publishing released Tiger's book on *Run and Shoot Football: Offense of the Future* to coaches in their book club. They had printed only ten thousand copies, since sales in the small niche market of the coaches' sports genre did not typically sell in large quantities. However, within a year and a half, they were into their third printing, and at forty-four thousand copies, the book was the best seller in the category that they had ever had by far. The game was rapidly growing more complex, and coaches at all levels were hungry for new schemes that could give them an offensive advantage and make their teams more productive on the scoreboard.

Except Woody Hayes. He continued to have mediocre seasons, and in 1966 he turned in his second losing season since assuming the helm at Ohio State. His moods became more truculent as he was forced to think about change. Local fans and alumni from across the country were becoming more than a little restless with the coach of their big-time bastion of first-class football, and small aircraft started appearing out of nowhere flying "Bye Bye Woody" banners all around the city and over the Horseshoe Stadium. Attendance began to drop off for the first time, and rumors began to spread that Woody's tenure might be in jeopardy.

But Woody Hayes was a warrior. He felt all the more determined in his role, and was sure that the recruiting program they had put in place a few years earlier was going to pay off. They were once again beginning to feed outstanding talent into their program. For three years, the coaching staff had been pursuing a full-court press to find the best high school talent in the northeastern part of the United States. That was about all the territory they could personally cover. This was their counteroffensive to those other schools that continued to raid Ohio of its homegrown talent. Tiger and the other assistant coaches from Ohio would pound the pavement within the state to persuade the best to come to Columbus, while Woody and his defensive coordinator, Lou McCullough, would comb the cities of New York and New Jersey, and the countryside of Virginia and West Virginia, to entice those boys from the East to come to Ohio. But it would take a while for the payout to come.

There is little doubt that the tipping point for Woody's stubborn intransigence about opening up the offense came in 1967, when the Purdue Boilermakers rolled into Ohio Stadium and proceeded to put on the most sensational and productive aerial display that Ohio State fans had ever seen. Much to their dismay, they watched in awe as Purdue's fleet-of-foot quarterback Mike Phipps filled the stadium airways with flying pigskins, and led his team to a 41-6 trouncing over the stunned Buckeyes. Purdue had taken the Run and Shoot concepts into their arsenal, and were producing sensational results with it.

In the locker room after the crushing defeat, Woody went ballistic, slamming his left paw into the lockers and roaring, "Damn it to hell, we've got to *do* something!" Players and coaches alike gave him a wide berth. Tiger, while standing far enough away so one of those blows didn't land on him, said, "Damn right, Woody, we need to Run and Shoot!" The Boilermakers would make Woody boil for most of the coming year!

But Woody Hayes was a complex study in contrasts. As cranky as he could get with his coaches and players, he still consistently went out of his way to demonstrate his personal generosity and loyalty to all those around him who served under his command.

Woody and I were talking one night about our kids who were both enrolled at Ohio State. They were both majoring in math, and Steve wanted to go to law school after that. My daughter CJ wanted to go to law school, too, but our financial plans had not included three more years of college for her. And

even though she was scholastically gifted, girls really didn't get scholarships in those days, especially when they were competing with boys.

Elsie and I had raised our girls to be teachers, a noble profession, and one particularly suited to women who wanted to marry and raise kids. It was perfect because their schedules would be exactly the same as their youngsters.

But CJ decided she wanted to major in pure math and then become a systems engineer, whatever that meant. We named her Carolyn Joyce, and she did seem to take after my sister Joyce with her penchant for math. Who knows why; math has no heartbeat! But she was a "Thinking Man's Woman."

Now, my mama raised two teachers, two lawyers, two administrative assistants, two commercial artists, and one PhD in research physics. There was not a systems engineer or corporate type among them. So Woody and I talked about that one night, and he took it upon himself to call a neighbor of his on Cardiff Avenue, Terry Lowrey, who worked for Bell Labs on the west end of town.

The next day he told me Terry not only knew what a systems engineer was, but he had a bunch of them working for him. Even though he had no budget that year for summer interns, he'd be happy to talk to her about the profession.

Well, what do you know! Terry was so impressed with my baby girl he offered her a summer job anyway, and told Woody she could work for the Labs anytime! I guess a girl *could* compete with men in a corporate profession.

Woody Hayes was privately interested in the well-being of those around him, always actively helping players, coaches, friends, even total strangers. CJ had helped him with tutoring some of his players through their math and science classes, so Woody wanted to give something back to her. Carolyn Joyce Ellison graduated from Ohio State with a math major, and joined IBM as a systems engineer. She retired from her corporate career as vice president of Strategic Planning and Human Resources for the European Operations of a large U.S. multinational. She always told those who worked for her that they had to get off the sidelines and into the game because there was never any substitute for performance. "You can spend your days analyzing the politics of it all, but the best way to succeed is to simply 'Hit 'em where it hurts! On the scoreboard, baby!'"

12

BABY BUCKS AND THE BIG BOWL OF ROSES

In the week following the shellacking that the Buckeyes received at the skillful hands of Purdue in 1967, Tiger saw Woody sitting in his office, alone and brooding and frenetically tapping a pen in overtime on the desk. He decided to go in and try to have a conversation with him, man-to-man and eyeball-to-eyeball. They had had many such conversations through the years, but the stakes for Woody were as high as they had ever been.

"Woody, you know this offense has served you well through the years. But our opponents have it so well scouted by now that they could shut it down in their sleep. We need to surprise them with something new. We have the talent on this team to do it now, and when we pour the freshmen into the mix next year, you'll have yourself a team capable of stunning the nation with its productive, skillful, mobile, fan-pleasing football."

Of course, you never knew whether Woody would sit and talk with you about a situation, or bellow and blow up. The tension of this moment was no exception as he stared holes through me, but I figured that what I had said was exactly what was on his mind. He finally barked, "Damn it to hell, Tiger, I'm the head coach here and I know what the problem is. What the hell makes you think you know so much?" I could see the frustration and angst on his snarly face, so I said, "I just KNOW, by my NOSE, and my TWO BIG TOES." And I left him alone in his misery.

Within a matter of seconds, he padded into my office and sat down. "Tiger, you know I can't completely change my offense in midseason. This is the offense we coached and practiced, and this is what our boys know. But I also know if I'm ever going to take the plunge, the timing and talent we've lined up for next year are right on the money for it.

"I think we better get ourselves a few new young coaches in here in the spring and add some dimension to this offense. In the meantime, we need to focus on toughing it out and winning games for the rest of the season. We especially need to beat that school up north." I couldn't have agreed more.

As he was leaving, he turned around in a quandary and said, "What the hell was that about your nose and your toes?" I chuckled and told him it was just something my mom used to say when it seemed there was no better explanation at the time.

It was clear that no one needed to explain the gravity of the situation to Woody. Every coach on our staff knew what we had in the freshmen hopper for the following year, but if we didn't pull a rabbit out of the hat for the remainder of this season, we might not be around to coach that terrific bunch of kids. Since the Michigan Wolverines were also having a lackluster season that year, the conventional wisdom of the day was that the outcome of the traditional season-ending game between these two powerhouse rivals would determine which of the two head coaches would be dealt a career-ending defeat.

Tiger, forever the master of the melodic metaphor, had taken to calling his freshmen players the Baby Bucks. In 1967, however, the term became an ironic understatement to describe the size, speed, savvy, spirit, and poise that this talented class of young men brought to the game. They were smart, skilled, and hungry to show their stuff against the varsity team in practice. Many of their opponents' offensive playbooks were a lot more innovative than Ohio State's, so Tiger was able to teach the Baby Bucks some Run and Shoot maneuvers, like choosing a play based on the varsity's defensive set, or making cut adjustments—left or right, long or short, depending on what the defender did after the snap—or scrambling out of the pocket and passing on the run. So not only were the Baby Bucks able to give the varsity a look at the offense they would be facing in the upcoming game, but they were in many cases executing those plays better than their opponents would be on game day. And everyone on the varsity and coaching staff knew it.

Quarterback Rex Kern described it this way: "We would practice against the varsity defense in 1967, and one day illustrates what kind of talent we had. We were in goal-line offense, and the defensive coordinator, Lou McCullough, and our freshman coach, Tiger Ellison, were going back and forth.

"'OK, this is what Purdue is going to be running on the goal line,' Lou told Tiger. 'Let's see if you can score on us.'

"We gave it to John Brockington, and he would score without anybody touching him. 'OK, let's see what the Baby Bucks can do from the 3-yard line,' Lou shouted. So they moved it back to the 3-yard line, and we gave it to Larry Zelina and he scored. They moved it back to the 6, and we scored again. Tate [Jack Tatum] would score. Then Leo Hayden. They couldn't stop us. Now Lou's starting to get upset. 'Dang it, Tiger, you're not running the play right; you are not blocking this the way you are supposed to,' he yelled.

"Tiger would just say, 'You can't stop our Baby Bucks!'

"Earle Bruce was coaching the defensive backs that season, and he had this tackling drill for them where they had a five-yard square. They would line up, three defensive backs in this square, and give the ball to the freshmen and they would have to tackle [the freshmen]. First Zelina, and he would get by all three. Brock would run right over them. [Ron] Maciejowski would get through. Tate made it look easy. I would make it. Earle would get so upset with those defensive backs, but they couldn't tackle us. Some of them couldn't touch us."[13]

Since freshmen were not eligible to play on the varsity team in those days, Woody and all his coaches knew they needed to pound out the rest of the '67 season, just to have the privilege of coaching this group of guys who brought such extraordinary talent and poise to the game. The season had started with a disappointing 2-3 record, but through old-fashioned grind-it-out toughness, they finished the year 6-3. And they defeated their archrival from up north. Michigan coach Bump Elliott was given one more year to get his program back on track, but little did he know what he would be facing in the Buckeyes when they took the field in 1968. And General Hayes and company stayed to play yet one more day, in command of what was to become the best team any of them had ever coached.

At the Football Banquet after the season, Woody asked Tiger to give the keynote speech, and with his usual oratorical vigor, he had the Quarterback Clubbers and media focused on the great season comeback for the Buckeyes. At the end, he introduced his freshmen, with the following caveat: "Folks, these are the lads we call the Baby Bucks. But I want you to know, men of the varsity, that next fall they will become the Super Sophomores.

---

[13] Jim Tressel, *What It Means To Be a Buckeye*, Edited by Jeff Snook (Chicago: Triumph Books, 2003), pp 85-86

And, fellas, *they are hot to earn your spot!*" The room erupted in enthusiastic applause and cheering, except from the varsity players, whose enthusiasm was a bit more tepid. They knew the drills those freshmen had put them through in practice that season.

That January Woody hired three new young coaches to assist with the varsity, and the blend of talent and experience would turn out to give Ohio State one of the strongest complements of coaches ever assembled in the college ranks. Young Lou Holtz had been hired to help out with the defensive backs, and came to his first coaches' meeting ready to roll up his sleeves and get to work. But as he entered the room, he discovered Woody had already rolled up his sleeves and was punching out an assistant coach over an altercation about a player's grade point average. The other coaches, including 150-pound Holtz, jumped into the fray to pull them apart. They were off to quite a start, but that was just for openers.

Woody settled down and welcomed the new coaches to the staff, giving them a history lesson on Patton's military strategy in World War II as if nothing out of the ordinary had happened. He drilled them on how Patton didn't want his men to love him, he wanted them to fight! They would have the best conditioning for endurance, and the best fundamentals for winning every battle, and they would go on to total victory! Just like the Buckeyes! But then a little later he became agitated at something else and picked up a film projector with both hands, hurling it across the room and sending it crashing through the glass of the conference room door. At that point, he suggested they take a little break so his secretary could get the shattered glass and mangled projector pieces cleaned up and out of the way.

Lou describes the drama of his first day on the job this way: "As I stretched my aching legs and exited the room with my head down, the only thought rumbling like a train through my head was, 'Oh my god, Lou, what have you gotten yourself into?'

"Then I heard one of the coaches behind me singing a popular Bobby Russell song: 'God didn't make little green apples / and it don't rain in Indianapolis / in the summertime.' I turned and saw our troubadour, Tiger Ellison, the man who had assured me that Coach Hayes was 'overall a good guy, and a great leader.'

"'Tiger, how can you be singing?' I said.

"'I just open my mouth and the melody comes out.'

"'Well, that's just wonderful, but didn't you see what just happened in there?'

"He laughed and put a hand on my shoulder. 'Don't worry about it, son. You'll get used to it.'

"Oh, no! He'd just said I would get used to fistfights and flying projectors!

"'Tiger, I thought you said Coach Hayes was a good guy, a great leader?'

"He chuckled again. 'Hey, Attila the Hun was a great leader. Doesn't mean you'd have him over for dinner.'

"That's when I realized I'd been snookered. Coach Hayes had kept me away from every assistant coach except Tiger Ellison because Tiger had never said an unkind word about anybody in his life. The guy even found a way to compliment Attila the Hun! Coach Hayes knew this, so he let Tiger be the recruiting spokesman."[14]

It would take Lou a while to learn what Tiger already knew about his longtime friend, that Woody would often use his volatile rage to emphasize a point. He also knew that Woody had already come to the reluctant conclusion that he must add some innovation and surprise to his offensive strategy. And even though Woody and Tiger had spent many a late night discussing the philosophy and wisdom of a balanced run and shoot attack, and the deceptive value of spreading the offense and putting a man in motion to make the defense adjust and commit early, while he may have agreed intellectually, his visceral instincts were on unfamiliar turf here. General Hayes was not comfortable in unfamiliar territory, and his temperamental swings were amplified by the uncertainty he was brooding over: a new offensive strategy, three new coaches who were untested in this pressure-cooker environment, and all those young Bucks who would most likely be filling out the varsity roster as Super Sophomores the next season. In his heart he still believed sophomores could never handle the level of Big Ten competition like the seasoned battle-worn veterans.

When they regrouped for the afternoon, Woody strode to the blackboard and wrote "ROBUST" in big letters, and began to recite the gospel of the full-house backfield offense that characterized seventeen years of Ohio State football under his command. His gut instincts would always cling to what he knew best until he tested the mettle of those in the room, and no sale was ever going to be made without a good fight. Fresh ideas were great, but he wanted to plumb the depths of his coaches' expertise and conviction before committing to a more complex strategy.

George Chaump, the young new quarterback coach, had come to the staff from Harrisburg, Pennsylvania, where he had led his high school teams to four consecutive undefeated seasons and state championships, using the I-formation. Next to Tiger, he probably knew better than anybody else the range of talent and sophistication that the Baby Bucks would be

---

[14] Lou Holtz, *Wins, Losses, and Lessons* (New York: William Morrow, HarperCollins Publishers, 2006), pp 91-92

bringing into the next season because he had spent his first few weeks on the job analyzing the freshmen game film while the other coaches were out recruiting. Being reasonably undaunted by flying fists and flying electronics, he listened intently to Woody's uninterrupted monologue for as long as he could, and finally raised his hand. "Coach, do you really think this straight T-formation takes the best advantage of the incredible range of skill we have on this team?"

George and I had discussed each of those guys at length, and I knew he was salivating at the thought of putting them into a well orchestrated I or slot-I. Woody's offense had them bunched up shoulder to shoulder like a big Mac truck in the middle of the field, and that just made Chaump crazy! George was a darned good coach and really knew his stuff when it came to this kind of offense. So what ensued for the next hour or so was this back and forth, with Woody firing questions at him like a drill sergeant, and Chaump respectfully and knowledgably coming right back at him with answers.

I was silently smiling to myself as I watched the exchange, hoping Woody had already vented his daily dose of dread earlier, and wondering how the young coach's fresh ideas about the more complex and mobile approach were landing on the Old General. As Woody's intensity escalated, so did Chaump's energetic explanations, and we could see the pressure cooker start to blow. Finally he thundered, "Damn it to hell, Chaump, you've never coached a minute of college football in your life! As long as I'm the head coach of football at Ohio State, *nobody* is going to take away my fullback play! And you're trying to tell me your power-off-tackle play is better than the fullback play?"

Chaump said emphatically: "Coach, there is no comparison!" Well, that was it! Woody exploded, told him to get out; he was fired. George hesitated because he wasn't sure if the Old Man was serious, but then decided he had better get out so he wouldn't get punched out! See, being a newbie to the staff, he didn't realize we all got fired several times a year, at least for about twenty seconds, until Woody's blinding rage dissipated and he moved on.

So after twenty seconds, Woody stuck his head out the door and told the coach to get back in the room. Then he sat down and stared into blank space, brooding for about five minutes. The oxygen was sucked out of the air as we waited. In my mind the confluence of events was complete: the previous season that had nearly cut us all out of the pattern; the promising

payout of a successful recruiting strategy that had brought such talent to the team; and now, the demonstrated conviction and expertise of his entire coaching staff, all pointing to just one conclusion: now or never. But Woody was Woody!

Finally our consummate gentleman and diplomat, Hugh Hindman, allowed as how he liked what he heard and thought we ought to go with it. Earle Bruce joined in and said he believed that with the talent we had, it was a winning strategy that could take us all the way. Young Rudy Hubbard rounded out the offensive staff, and he said he thought the new look would capitalize on our strengths and frustrate the opponents' defenses all to hell. I just couldn't help myself, I pumped my fist in the air and bellowed, "Yahoo! Shades of Run and Shoot!"[15]

Woody finally crossed over the chasm of his own brooding morass, and conceded to add some innovation to the Ohio State arsenal. He told the coaches to order in game film from other big schools that were using the I-formation successfully and to clear all their calendars and be prepared to burn the midnight oil for a few weeks because they needed to analyze, graph and select the play series to fill out the new playbook before the boys reported for spring practice. He even conceded to add a few strategies from Tiger's gospel of Run and Shoot: six plays from the Gangster series, the option of using a no-huddle offense to wear down opponents' defenses, and granting the quarterback the freedom to call plays based on what he saw across the line of scrimmage. But through it all he made it clear that ROBUST was still the core of his offense, and in short yardage and goal line situations they would stay with their power plays. He wasn't about to turn his historically powerful fullback into just a glorified blocking guard in what he still suspected was a lighthouse offense.

Woody made one other concession to his staff that year. At the urging of his defensive coordinator, Lou McCullough, he reluctantly agreed to split the best talent from the soon-to-be Super Sophomores between offense and defense. Always before, he had picked the best players for offense, and given the AYOs—the All You Others—to defense. With the depth of the talent at every position, McCullough convinced him to alternate picks that year, in order to create a championship-caliber defense to match the promising new strategy and skill set on offense. That is how high school

---

[15] For a perspective from the other coaches and players, see Steve Greenberg and Larry Zelina, *Ohio State '68: All the Way to the Top* (Champaign, IL: Sports Publishing, 1998)

All Star offensive players like Jack Tatum and Mike Sensibaugh and Tim Anderson ended up playing defense for Ohio State.

As they went into spring practice, the level of intensity of the practice sessions elevated beyond anything the boys had ever experienced. The coaches pushed them to perfection in the fundamentals of blocking and tackling, executing the extended playbook over and over, working them beyond all previous limits, making them run sprints every day after regular practice so they would be in top condition. And at the conclusion of spring practice, twelve of the Baby Bucks were selected to fill out the starting roster for the varsity team in the fall. Energy levels ran high as every coach and player recognized the talent and commitment these boys had to each other and their school. They sensed they were part of something special: great leadership, incredible talent and depth at every position, the chemistry and camaraderie that inspire a team to excel, an individual and collective will to win that would not be denied.

I remember in the fall, all that the defensive coaches wanted the scout team to run against the varsity was the Purdue offense, from late summer practice into the third week of the regular season. We had two nonconference games before that, but McCullough, Holtz, Bill Mallory, and Esco Sarkkinen had spent their entire summer studying Purdue game film and obsessing over a complex defense to shut them down. Now we had SMU for our season opener and they were a fluid Run and Shoot team, spread 'em out across the field and pass on the quick drop, tough to defend. So a few times we got a little creative in our interpretation of what the coaches thought Purdue was going to give them, and showed them what else was possible from Purdue if they wanted to surprise us with some more razzle-dazzle Run and Shoot!

However, I have to tell you, the defensive coaches had those guys so well prepared and pumped up that they weren't about to let anything get past them. And the five Super Sophs starting on defense were playing as tough and smart as any veterans we'd ever had. Jim Stillwagon at middle guard was about as good as it gets. Jack Tatum was lightning fast and as tough as they come at linebacker. Mark Debevc at right end and Timmy Anderson at right half practiced like men inspired and were topnotch. Mike Sensibaugh, a former high school All Star quarterback, took to the safety position like a mountain cougar on the prowl.

Ohio State won its two nonconference games at the beginning of that year, primarily on the strength of the defense, even though SMU gained more than 430 offensive yards on them in the first game, setting an NCAA record with seventy-six passes. But the Buckeye defense rose to the occasion whenever it counted the most. The offense relied primarily on Woody's power-T, while occasionally throwing in one of the innovative I-formation plays from Chaump's additions to the repertoire. Woody's powerful fullback that year was the talented Jim Otis, and Woody's trademark offense came to be known as "Three yards and Otis" in the years he held that position for the Bucks.

But when the Purdue Boilermakers rolled into town for the third game, ranked number one in the country by every poll, and having scored more than forty points per game that season with All American quarterback Mike Phipps and Heisman Trophy contender Leroy Keyes leading the way, Woody and the Buckeyes pulled out all the stops. Their sights had been set on this team for ten months, and they were determined to shut them down at all costs. The Buckeyes came out with a no-huddle offense and stayed with it the whole game, using hand signals to communicate with their wideouts and wearing down Purdue's huge defensive line in the process. They combined their traditional power game with so much innovation and deception, that the fans in the Horseshoe were gasping in disbelief, incredulous that they were actually watching their beloved "romp-'em-stomp-'em" Buckeyes moving the ball down the field like a gaggle of graceful gazelles. Once again the defense played like men inspired, cleverly changing up their coverage whenever they noticed the quarterback keying off certain sets.

Woody invited four-star General Lew Walt, Commandant of the United States Marine Corps, to give the boys a pep talk in the locker room at half time. He spoke about the brave warriors in the trenches of Vietnam fighting for their cause, and compared that to the mission of the Buckeyes that day. Many of those young men had high school friends who were serving or had given their lives in Vietnam, and by the time they were ready to return to the field, there was not one dry eyeball to be found among players or coaches as they stormed out of the locker room for the second half.

The third quarter saw every player on the Buckeye squad elevate his game. They pumped each other up as the defense broke the rhythm of Purdue's offense with superior pursuit and tackling and interceptions and recovered fumbles, and the offense tirelessly executed with no huddle, wearing down the defense and maneuvering with authority as they closed Purdue out 13-0. It was a stunning victory. The fans reacted as if they had just won the National Championship, and some would later say that's exactly what happened that day in defeating the number one team in the country. It was a turning point. The Buckeyes had gotten a taste of what it feels like to play at the top of the game, and not one of them wanted to play football for anything less from that point on.

No game was ever easy for the Buckeyes the rest of the season, but even great teams have to win a few of them ugly in order to become champions. They were undefeated as their archrival from Ann Arbor came into Ohio Stadium to play the traditional season finale. The Buckeyes' adrenalin was squirting on overtime as they took the field because only Michigan stood in the way of their chance at the National Championship title and a big bowl of roses. They dominated the game from the very beginning and soundly defeated the Wolverines 50-14. The young Bucks were elated! They had grown up together during that season, and were exuberant as they prepared to head for the Promised Land of Pasadena, California, in search of a National Title.

The victory over Michigan had come on November 23, 1968, and the Rose Bowl would not be played until January 1, 1969. To keep the edge on the team's fighting spirit and get them ready for sunny Southern California, Woody ran the practices in the French Field House with the thermometer cranked up to 98 degrees. With fourteen pounds of football armor draped on their bodies, the gridiron warriors found this treatment brutal, especially since the snow outside in Columbus was ankle deep. But by the time they got to Pasadena, and practiced with the hot California sun scorching down on them and the Los Angeles smog hanging low and heavy on the practice field, they were grateful for the preparation.

Three days before game day was "hump" day, the last hard practice before taking the field for the big one. Every coach knows you win each football game twice, once in practice on hump day, and then on the playing field on game day. But Woody thought the men were practicing lazy, and he went crazy. "Southern California. In the Rose Bowl. For the National Championship. And you're LOAFING! Every one of you is LOAFING! One hundred thousand people in the stands all about us are watching us, the Ohio State Buckeyes. One hundred million more around this nation with their eyes glued to their television sets watching us, the Ohio State Buckeyes, going for the National Championship, and what are they seeing? Lazy men, LOAFING! Captain Dave Foley! Captain Dirk Worden! Get over here, right here, beside me. Now tell these youngsters what they have to do!"

The senior co-captains, the old men of the squad, stood in the center of the circle and let their blazing eyes pan each individual, telegraphing the intensity of raging bulls coming eyeball-to-eyeball with the scarlet shirts of the young squad. This was the gang of adrenalin-squirting upstarts who had grabbed the Big Ten Title and had come storming to the West Coast hungry for the National Championship. Today they were hungry for nothing. They were loafing. There was certain defeat simmering under the hot California sun on the practice field that day.

The electricity arced between the oldsters and the youngsters, until the Captains finally pounded their fists into their palms and shouted, "We've got to SOCK IT TO 'EM! KNOCK 'EM DOWN! HIT! *Play today like your life depends on it because it does! You will NOT be able to live with yourselves if you don't give it EVERYTHING you've got!*"

For the next hour and a half, those young men went at each other hammer and tongs, tooth and toenail, and when the day was over, they wobbled into the locker room on aching dogs that could hunt no more. But the next day they sprang back into action, the following day they oozed a little more perspiration, and on New Years Day they stormed into the Rose Bowl and got what they came for.

The game was not always pretty. In the first half, USC went up 10-0, after Heisman Trophy winner O. J. Simpson slipped tackles and elusively ran for an 80-yard touchdown.

I was standing on the left side of Woody, which was always a mistake because he was left-handed. As OJ ran crooked and sideways and slippery across and down the field to the goal line, I got a WHOP! Right between the shoulder blades! I thought I'd been kicked by a Georgia mule.

I went down on all fours and then jumped back up and jumped right in Woody's face, and he said, "Did I hit 'ya, Tiger?" And I said, "You're damn right you hit me!" And he put his arm around my shoulder and said, "Hey, it's a good thing that damned son of a gun finally stopped, or else he might have drowned out there in the Pacific Ocean!"

But I can tell you, after that, the kids regrouped and reached deep. There was serious intensity about them as they mustered their determination to step up to the challenge and win.

Sophomore Rex Kern was the most gifted run and shoot quarterback I had ever coached. He was fast and strong, and a natural leader on the field, seeing lanes open up, scrambling to avoid the rush, calling plays at the line of scrimmage if he didn't like what the defense was giving him for the play called in the huddle. And he had that unshakable will to fight for his goal.

That day every man on the field became a real winner deep down inside himself. The defense played the best they had all year, and they were already the best in the country. The offense matured before our eyes as they came back to win that game 27-16. Every man on that team demonstrated a spirit

that would successfully carry him through life and inspire many a young person to follow in those footsteps.

"The greatest college football team during the decade of the '60s," is what Bud Wilkinson and his sports committee said of that Buckeye team. After the game was over, the players and coaches spent a day and a half celebrating their magnificent victory and enjoying the sights of Southern California. Then Woody Hayes boarded a military plane with General Lew Walt and made his fourth tour of Vietnam to visit the troops. The young assistant coaches wanted to stay on the West Coast to attend the annual meeting of the American Football Coaches Association in Los Angeles the following week, so they went to Las Vegas to celebrate and have some fun. Tiger and Elsie flew home with the players, whose adrenalin from the thrill of victory had been running on overtime as they savored the National Championship Title. No jet lag on this trip! And their energy was only fortified when they were greeted by thousands of faithful fans from the Buckeye Nation as they deplaned on the tarmac in Columbus.

The next morning Elsie had to get back to teaching her fifth-grade class at Worthington's Wilson Hills Elementary, and Tiger was left in quiet reflective surroundings for the first time in months. He could not keep a silly grin from engulfing his face as he relived the visions of those fine young men performing so brilliantly and earning themselves a place in football history.

He threw on some sweats and a heavy jacket, and ran through the slushy snow for about two hours. When he returned, his mind consciously reflected on a time so many years earlier, when he, as a thirteen-year-old boy, sat in front of his Pop's radio in the living room, listening to the crackling voice of the announcer reading the ticker-tape play-by-play of another great Rose Bowl victory. Knute Rockne and his Four Horsemen had won the Rose Bowl in 1925, and for Tiger Ellison that was the beginning of a lifetime journey that had just been rewarded on a grand scale. At age fifty-eight, he had accomplished the goal set early in his lifetime, and it seemed that lifetime had gone by all too fast. But how great the rewards had been! It was time to set a new goal for the rest of his life.

As fate would have it, on New Year's Day of 1969, there was another young teenage boy from Ohio, watching the Rose Bowl game on his Pop's television in the family room as the Ohio State Buckeyes defeated USC for the National Championship. The next day, he saw on the front page of the *Cleveland Plain Dealer* a picture of a smiling Rex Kern, holding the Rose Bowl MVP football in one hand and a Bible in the other. The lad was struck by the wholesome integrity and natural leadership that Rex displayed at such a young age. Rex Kern became a hero to him, and he decided he wanted to coach football and inspire a team of players to become the best they could be, just as the Buckeyes had been that season. His father was a coach and he knew it to be a noble profession. Unbeknownst to that young teenager named Jim Tressel, he would realize his goal thirty-four years later, as he led his 2002 Ohio State Buckeyes to their first National Championship since the 1968 team had achieved it so many years earlier.[16]

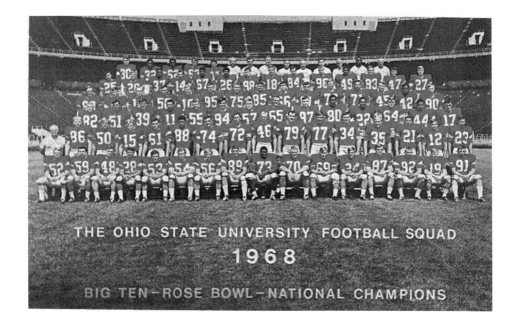

---
[16] Jim Tressel, "We are Family" in the *Ohio State Alumni Magazine*, Jan-Feb 2006

13

THE EVOLUTION OF THE GAME

When Tiger and Elsie Ellison were married in 1938, Elsie had been required to drop out of her chosen profession, since the Middletown School System did not permit married women to teach at that time. But when World War II came along, and men were being drafted into the armed forces by the tens of thousands, social policy was forced to change out of necessity, as a whole range of occupations were clamoring for women to join the workforce and fill the void left by the departing servicemen. With Tiger's support, Elsie chose to resume her teaching after her youngest child entered kindergarten.

That meant that in 1969, Tiger had spent thirty-five years in the Ohio Teachers System, and Elsie twenty-five, and they were at a decision point in their lives. They both loved their work and had found teaching and coaching young people personally rewarding. It had been quite a run! But now their pensions were fully vested, and they had the option to pursue other goals and dreams while their health was still good.

Being an assistant coach for five years at Ohio State had provided Tiger a chance to work with some of the finest young athletes in the country. And as he looked at the gold National Championship ring on his finger, the only piece of jewelry he'd ever owned in his life, he wasn't sure how he could improve upon that coaching experience. Instead, as an older coach, he was looking forward to helping younger coaches benefit from what he had learned about improving the great game of American football, and expanding upon all the possibilities that he visualized for the offense of the future. He wanted to continue conducting clinics and making speeches, and he had also been approached by Parker Publishing to write another book for coaches, this one a public speaking guide for how to use the power of the podium to persuade and inspire. Elsie also had some ideas about a book for grade-schoolers, one that would give math and science a heartbeat and make it fun for kids to learn. They both came to the decision that the time was right for them to move on at this stage of their lives. It would be an exciting adventure for them. Tiger would need to talk to Woody about their decision when he returned.

Tiger went to the Athletic Offices in St. John Arena that first week in January of 1969, still smiling to himself and savoring the great victory of their young team. The place was eerily quiet in comparison to all the hoopla of the preceding days in California. All the other assistant coaches were still on the West Coast, and Woody was still in Vietnam. He greeted his secretary Sandy Mazei, who was busy decorating the corridors and conference rooms with all the inevitable bounty that comes from great victory: television sets, golf clubs, dozens of fruit baskets, silver services, and plaques—all sorts of things donated by the grateful alumni, businesses, and loyal fans of the Buckeye Nation to express their thrill at their team's victory. It seemed the town was once again flying high over their beloved team and its coaches and players. "Bye Bye Woody" banners were nowhere to be found flying high over the city, and had been replaced by "Buckeye National Champs '68" banners.

Sandy came into my office to tell me that Paul Brown was on the phone. He had just started the Cincinnati Bengals expansion franchise the season before, so I picked up and said, "Hi, Paul. How is life treating you in Cincinnati?"

He chuckled and hummed a few bars about the woes of a startup team. But I knew Paul to be a great coach and organizer, one of the handful of brilliant leaders who had really brought professionalism to the game in the early years at the pro level. So I told him I knew the Bengals were in good hands and it wouldn't be long before we'd be seeing them high on the charts. Then Paul said, "I called to congratulate you, Tiger."

That gave me a chance to sing a few choruses of my own about our young team, and how they would most likely be even better in the '69 season. I didn't mention anything about leaving the organization; out of respect for Woody, he would be the first to know. But then Paul said, "Well, congratulations on that championship, too. But I was referring to your

book on *Run and Shoot Football.* It's a very creative approach, Tiger, and any coach worth his salt needs to pay attention to your ideas. There's a lot of food for thought, and I suspect it will be making offenses much more complex in the future."

I really appreciated a compliment like that coming from a legendary coach like Paul Brown. I was reinforced about taking on my new mission, so I suggested there might be some useful application of Run and Shoot concepts for an expansion team at the pro level. Food for thought!

When Woody returned to the office the following week, he and Tiger went over to the Faculty Club for a bite of lunch so they could talk uninterrupted. Tiger wanted to let him know of his decision to leave Columbus so Woody would have time to bring another coach onto the staff before recruiting trips and spring practice started absorbing all his time. They discussed his Vietnam trip, and how Woody had taken down the names and addresses of all those men he had visited. On the return flight home, he had already begun dictating into his tape recorder the letters he would be sending to loved ones of each of those men, with the personal messages of their conversations, and his hope for their safe return once their mission had been accomplished.

This was just the kind of person Woody was, a complex character whom the public only saw as ill-tempered and rigorously demanding on the sidelines, but who would privately take his own time to reach out to men on the battlefield and do whatever he could to give them inspiration. He used to tell the players that they could never give back and repay all those who had a hand in helping them become who they were. But they could always "give forward," by helping others along the way, and that's how they could pay back, by paying forward.

So in that vein, he provided me a great segue, and I said, "Woody, you've always talked about paying forward, and I share that philosophy with you. So Elsie and I have decided to pay forward to the professions we have enjoyed so much. We each have books we want to write, and I want to spend more time helping the young coaches absorb the possibilities of the Run and Shoot philosophy to advance the great game of football. We will be retiring at the end of the school year and moving to Florida."

I had never personally witnessed Woody's window of rage being suppressed, as it somewhat needed to be in the hallowed confines of the Faculty Club, and for a moment I thought he was going to explode or have a heart attack trying to contain it. He started pounding his left fist into his thigh, and finally said through clenched jaws, "Damn it, Tiger, don't do this now. You've pushed me to open up the offense for five years, and now that I have, this team is going to be even better next season than this one. This is not the time to walk away." Woody could not begin to imagine life without coaching.

I said, "Woody, I am not walking away, I'm walking proudly forward into the next phase of my life. Hey, buddy, I'm a teacher at heart, and I think I have more left to contribute to our profession by giving it forward to the next generation of coaches coming up. I have a National Championship ring on my finger, thanks to you, and it doesn't get any better than Number One. This is the right time."

When he realized my decision was final, lunch became a little easier to swallow, and we spent the next couple hours reflecting on two careers that had been so rewarding for each of us, different in so many ways, but both in pursuit of the same ideals. We hoped that the young people growing up currently would have the same love of American democratic ideals, and the passion for preserving them, that we shared as old coaches.

In the three and a half years since its publication, Tiger's book on *Run and Shoot Football: Offense of the Future* was still in high demand and the subject of many inquiring discussions. Librarians were complaining that it was one of those books that most often walked away from the shelf and never found its way back to the library. The concepts he laid out were so complex and new, that they could not be grasped with one pass through the book. Over one hundred fifty coaches, who had already incorporated parts of the offensive scheme, had personally contacted Tiger with questions and feedback, and Run and Shoot football was showing up in high school and college programs all across the country.

Typical of the experience coaches were having with the *Offense of the Future* was that of Ed Baker, athletic director and head football coach at the Haverford High School in suburban Philadelphia. As a member of the coaches' book club, Ed received a copy of Tiger's book just as he was packing up to leave for his summer job as codirector and part owner of a youth camp in New Hampshire. He tossed the book into his bag, and that night after the evening meal, he began reading. "I could not put the book down until I finished it well after midnight. It was a great read, and chock full of new ideas for the offense.

"Several of my varsity athletes from the Haverford School served as counselors at summer camp with me. So the next day I took a quarterback and receiver up to the athletic field while the youngsters had 'rest hour' after lunch, and we started experimenting with something Tiger called the 'automatic pass.' It worked well.

"So for the next several days during 'rest hour' we continued to experiment with more of the concepts in the book. We had so much fun with it that within a couple of weeks, I decided to go with the Run and Shoot 'hook, line, and sinker' during the approaching fall season at the high school.

"Back in the Philadelphia area that fall, we won all of our football games, and a local sports editor tagged us as 'the MacBean Machine.' Our quarterback was Scott MacBean, and with our new offense and his natural ability, we garnered a lot of positive attention in the Greater Philadelphia area. Scott went on to Princeton, and as their starting quarterback his senior year, he led Princeton to the Ivy League Championship with Run and Shoot finesse."

Several years later, while serving as head football coach for Kalamazoo College in Michigan, Coach Baker put the same double slot offense to work with similar results. Following that season, he was invited to conduct a three-day clinic for high school coaches in the Chicago area. He would hold up his worn copy of Tiger's book and tell the coaches to order it; everything from the teaching philosophy and the conceptual framework to the playbook itself would be of value to them. One of the coaches from that clinic wrote to him at the conclusion of his next football season to thank him for introducing the Run and Shoot to him, and to announce that he had just completed his first undefeated season at his school. Said Ed Baker, "Tiger Ellison certainly did have a pervasive and positive influence on the modern game through the publication of his book. And how prophetic that he called it *Offense of the Future*, since some forty years later, the principles that he outlined are commonly found being used by coaches at all levels of the game today, including the NFL."[17]

Football offenses had always been evolving, since the very early days when they more resembled a disorderly rugby scrum than any of the sophisticated play we are accustomed to seeing today. As rules changed through the years to factor in safety and to make the game more exciting for fans to watch, formations and playbooks evolved to take advantage of each team's unique abilities to compete. But the underlying philosophy of the game remained the same for most of those years, pinioned in the ground game, with emphasis on power and strength and ball control. The forward pass was considered a necessary evil to be executed in late down

---

[17] Personal correspondence, Ed Baker to Bill Triick, March 11, 2005

situations, when large chunks of real estate had to be gained in order to maintain possession.

But in the 1950s, a fundamental shift in offensive philosophy began to infiltrate the game. Most often attributed to Sid Gilman as the father of the modern passing game, new emphasis was put on the forward pass as a designed, inherent part of a more balanced and structured attack. New innovations were introduced into starting formations and the design of plays that would stretch the field vertically and force defenders to react to the possibility of the long forward pass downfield. The passing game was characterized by the quarterback dropping back deep into the pocket, waiting for the designated receiver to run his route and get open in a one-on-one matchup. A premium was placed on quarterbacks with the arm strength to heave the ball long yardage, linemen and backs who could provide protection in the pocket, and receivers with the speed to execute their routes and hit their spots ahead of the opponent's defender.

When Tiger's book on *Run and Shoot Football: Offense of the Future* was published in the mid-1960s, another fundamental shift in offensive philosophy was introduced into the game. Even Woody Hayes said at the time, "I am sure every coach, regardless of the level in which he works, will profit from a study of the revolutionary ideas expressed in this book." There were several ideas that were characterized as revolutionary at the time. Tiger advocated stretching the field not only vertically, but also horizontally, sideline to sideline, forcing defenders to spread laterally as well, and opening up the field for running or passing. Every play could be either a run or a pass, on any down, in any field position. Since the formation did not trigger "run" or "pass," defenders had to be ready for either on any play.

It was the first time anyone had planned for automatic play call adjustments based on the specific set of the defense, and automatic route conversions based on a defender's movement after the snap. Each play keyed off a specific defender, and since both the quarterback and his receivers saw the same defensive key, both could make their automatic adjustments in unison, without a word being communicated. Tiger advocated early motion on every play, so defenses had to commit early to their strategy and telegraph their intentions. Every play had multiple receivers, so the quarterback had multiple looks for passing. He advocated the use of hand signals for the first time, to keep the game moving and defenses off balance.

The offense required precision timing in the step sequences of the quarterback and receivers. It included a series of short, quick pass plays that could neutralize a defensive line's weight or strength advantage, pick up the pace of the game, and use passes instead of runs in short yardage situations. The maneuver required exact coordination in the timing of steps executed by the quarterback and receiver—either a three-step or five-step drop by the quarterback and cut by the receiver so the ball could be released just as the receiver began his cut.

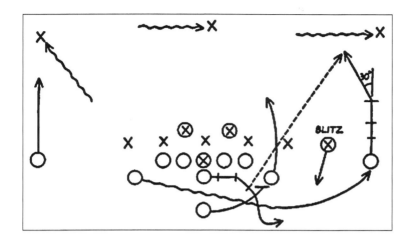

This offense put a premium on finesse, mobility and ball handling in all the skill positions. All were required to elevate their attention and make on-the-spot decisions. The quarterback needed to demonstrate the leadership ability to sense the action on the field, and the maneuverability to get the ball to any one of several receivers. His quick release and fine touch on the ball were of greater importance than arm strength, although with that additional weapon in the arsenal, the long pass downfield was an option on any play. Since many of the plays were designed for the quick, short-yardage pass, the distance run after the catch was often greater than the passing yardage itself.

All of these ideas were revolutionary in the 1960s. And in the years ahead, as coaches began to internalize the implications and combine them with their own strategies and formations, the complexity, productivity, and fan-pleasing nature of American football would escalate dramatically. As Rex Kern would say years later, "He was well ahead of his times as far as offensive football was concerned."[18]

Tiger and Elsie retired to Treasure Island, Florida, and enthusiastically began to enjoy life all over again. Tiger continued to make the rounds of the speaking circuit, which allowed them to travel around the country, and provided a pulpit for promoting the gospel according to Run and Shoot. They wrote their books, played tennis, took up golf, fished from their boat on the Boca Ciega Bay, answered phone calls and letters from coaches all

---

[18] *Buckeye Sports Bulletin* 9, no. 30 (August 1990)

across the country, and studied *Sports Illustrated* like a racing form, to stay on top of what was going on in America's greatest fighting game.

The revolution of the game at the professional level began to show up in 1970, as Tiger watched Paul Brown's Cincinnati Bengals responding to the devastating loss of their starting quarterback Greg Cook to a shoulder injury.

The year before, the Bengals had started this rookie quarterback Greg Cook out of the University of Cincinnati, and that kid was as strong, smart, and poised on the field as any veteran in the league. He could heave the forward pass sixty yards down the field and land it in a bushel basket if he had to, and he set all kinds of records that year. They were pretty much running an offense of the Sid Gilman variety.

When Cook injured his shoulder in 1970, they had to go with their backup quarterback Virgil Carter, an athletic, scrappy, agile guy, but not one with the arm strength that Cook had. As an expansion team in its third year, they still had a strength disadvantage at the line as well. That's when I noticed changes in their offensive strategy, to use more man-in-motion plays, spread multiple receivers, and short-to-medium quick passes to control the ball rather than relying on the running game. They won their division that year.

Creative ideas have to be planted in fertile soil if they are to germinate. It turns out Paul had a brilliant young offensive strategist in Assistant Coach Bill Walsh, who would become one of the best, most innovative coaches of the era. I was as surprised as anybody that Walsh wasn't tapped for the Bengals' head coaching job when Paul stepped down in 1975. But Walsh took his fantastic offense to the Chargers for a year, and turned Dan Fouts, a strict drop-back passer, into one of the most productive in the league, as he teamed up with his receivers in executing the San Diego pass offense according to Lonesome Polecat pass-cut principles. Then in San Francisco as head coach, he took the 49ers from the cellar to the Super Bowl three times in the '80s, with the incomparable Joe Montana as quarterback. Walsh was a "Thinking Man's Coach" who could stand shoulder-to-shoulder with the great ones in football history.

Bill Walsh's offense would come to be known as the West Coast Offense, inappropriately named since it was born on the West Coast of Southern Ohio in Cincinnati. But as the complexity of offenses proliferated, sportswriters and commentators were having trouble characterizing them like they used to, with simple names like Single Wing, I-formation, or Wish Bone. The West Coast Offense was run out of multiple formations, and better reflected a philosophy than a formation. The philosophical pinions were to stretch the field both vertically and horizontally, throw the ball on any down, replace many a rushing play with quick short-to-medium passes, precision timing between quarterback and receiver, and automatic adjustments keyed off a specific defender. Variations of this philosophy can currently be found in all NFL teams' offenses.

More than just the philosophy of Tiger's *Offense of the Future* would begin to infiltrate the ranks of the professional league in the years ahead, particularly under the leadership of Coach Darrell "Mouse" Davis and his associates. As the head football coach at Portland State in Oregon between 1975 and 1980, Coach Davis became a disciple of Tiger's Run and Shoot thinking, including his double-slot spread formation which featured two wide receivers, two backs in the slot, one running back who was also an eligible receiver, and no tight ends. From this formation, he selected and adapted a package of three running plays and five passing plays that would become the core of his offensive scheme. Instead of keying off a single specific defender, his players keyed off an entire defensive coverage, either the two-deep or three-deep zone, man-to-man, or blitz, then made their automatic adjustments accordingly. During those six years at Portland State, his quarterbacks June Jones and Neil Lomax dazzled the nation by setting all sorts of new NCAA offensive records at the Division II level of college ball.

In the '80s, Mouse Davis would take his offensive scheme to the Canadian Football League, where he coached the Toronto Argonauts to a Grey Cup Title, Canada's version of the Super Bowl. He then took it to the short-lived USFL Houston Gamblers, where the talented Jim Kelly blew the roof off all previous single-season pro records for passing yardage and total offense. In the late '80s, June Jones became quarterback coach for the Houston Oilers under Head Coach Jerry Glanville, where he introduced the Run and Shoot, and helped quarterback Warren Moon achieve an all-pro performance that would eventually break even more NFL records and propel him to the Professional Football Hall of Fame his first year of eligibility—the first black quarterback to achieve that honor. Mouse Davis, in the meantime, brought his Run and Shoot to the Detroit Lions, and Jerry Glanville moved to the Atlanta Falcons as head coach and introduced the offense there. So well into the mid-1990s, three NFL pro teams used Mouse Davis's Run and Shoot almost exclusively: Houston, Atlanta, and Detroit.

The media and sportscasters picked up on the name Run and Shoot to describe Mouse's version of the offense, and it became synonymous with the double-slot formation with no tight ends and Mouse's playbook. The spunky guy was unfortunately saddled with the name Run and Shoot, and he would write or call periodically and tell me that the commentators and reporters

kept challenging him as to whether he or Tiger Ellison actually invented the thing. He assured me he always gave me credit for the original.

Well, credit was not something I was looking for, and I truly admired what this scrappy young coach had done with the ideas in the *Offense of the Future*. He had internalized them and made them his own, which was the whole idea of the thing.

But as an old coach and teacher, I could not help advising him that I thought he needed to be running the ball more often, playing with more balance in the offense to keep the defenders on their toes and to manage the clock better. But I sure couldn't blame him for being enamored by the passing productivity of this Run and Shoot because he was getting record-breaking performances out of the thing! And it was fun, fan-pleasing football! Even the coach was having fun with it.

In the mid-1980s, Parker Publishing contacted Tiger about updating and reissuing his book, this time as *Run and Shoot Football: The Now Attack*. They were still getting demand for the old one, published twenty years earlier and by then out of print. And because a new generation of young coaches had entered the profession since that time, there was still a market for those new coaches who were eager to learn the intricacies and philosophy and possibilities that by now had taken the game by storm. Tiger was more than happy to take on the project, and looked forward to what this new wave of young minds would be able to do with the game in the years ahead.

There are those today who acknowledge that the Run and Shoot has made a difference in the offenses used by the little leagues, high schools and small colleges, but claim that it is no longer a viable offense at the powerhouse colleges or professional levels because the size, speed, and sophistication of the defenders in the game today make it untenable. But they are referring to Run and Shoot as the double-slot made famous by Mouse Davis and company. There is not a coach, player, or knowledgeable observer of Tiger's *Offense of the Future* turned *Now Attack*, who will not tell you that the concepts he introduced forty years ago are clearly present under all sorts of other names, and have become an integral part of modern offenses used in the great game of American football at all levels. Whenever you hear of Spread Offenses, or four-receiver sets, or defensive keys that trigger route conversions, or short-to-medium quick slant passes on the run, or tricky little run and pass plays that look alike and are executed on any down in any field position, or hand signals with no huddle, or defensive coordinators who are exasperated by the deception and productive skill of an opposing offense, you may be sure that the spirit of the Tiger is alive and well, pumping its fist and proclaiming, "Yahoo! Shades of Run and Shoot!"

14

REAL WINNERS

When Bob Hart retired from Ford Motor Company, and then from his alma mater, Miami University, he set about helping to organize a mentoring program for teenage boys in Middletown, Ohio in 2005. In doing so, he reflected on the key messages he had learned as a youngster on the gridiron of Middletown High School so many years earlier, and how those messages that had reverberated across the field had resonated with him throughout his life. He wanted to pay forward to the young people growing up today in his hometown so they too would have the benefit of the guidance that had served him so well in life.

"Tiger touched something deep in my soul decades ago, even as a young boy watching two-a-days at Barnitz Stadium. My own parents had given me a moral compass, and taught me the value of hard work. But for the most part it was all business, all work and no play, which for a youngster can lead to the idea that work is drudgery, something not to be joyful about, something that must be done just to please others.

"But Tiger demanded that you approach work with positive intensity, with the joy of pouring your spirit into it. Whatever worthwhile goal you set for yourself, you needed to go after it with everything in you, mind, body, and soul. I just had to be a part of that. He made everything about serious work seem like serious fun as well, filling the airwaves with expressions like, "Dig, little pig!" or "Pahhhh-tooey!" when directing conditioning drills or if something went wrong. Then we'd go after it all over again until we got it right, and, man, did it feel good to get it right! His positive energy was contagious because when we got it right, our own energy would ratchet up a notch and make anything seem possible. It was exciting, and it was fun!

"I think perhaps the most important lesson of all for young people, is to realize early on that they have the power within themselves to tap their own fighting spirit in the most positive way, and to use that energy to educate their minds and achieve worthy goals. If they give that power away, or wait for someone else to be the source of their energy, they will waste the greatest human gift we were ever given. If they reach for the best they have in them, and pour themselves into it, they will own the joyful and energizing experience of personal fulfillment. That's really all a man has at the end of his days, a personal accountability for how he used his own winning spirit. It is the toughest and most tested measure of the man, what he did with the life he was given, how he used his energy to strive and become better for himself and for others."

Tiger would often liken the fighting spirit inside a person to the electricity available from an outlet. It was pretty hard for most people to describe what electricity looked like, or to get their minds around the science of how it was generated. But a man could certainly realize the effects of tapping into it. If he plugged in and used it for positive purposes, it could make his life better. If he used his energy in the wrong way, just like electricity, it could hurt him or even get him killed. Harnessed toward positive, productive ends, the fighting spirit would make any person a real winner, regardless of the circumstances life may have thrown his way. And the real winner would attract the positive energy of others around him because a winning spirit has magnetic pull that attracts the best in others.

To coaches at the annual meeting of the American Football Coaches Association in 1964, Tiger explained it this way.

What is a real winner? I'll tell you what a real winner is. If we took all the men in this nation above eighteen years of age and piled them into three piles according to the kinds of men they are, we would have a little 10 percent pile which would say, "The Real Winner" on this one side, and on the other side we would have a 10 percent pile of our men with a sign, "The Real Loser," and then in the middle there would be a great mass of humanity, 80 percent of our men, with a sign that would say, "The Shoulder Shrugger." There is a difference.

Take one of these guys that we call the real winner and analyze him, throw the psychology book at him, study the boy. Notice that when he goes forth to do something he goes about it with a clear, vivid picture in his mind of

the thing he is fighting for, and at the same time he has an intense, burning desire in his heart to fight for it. When he is successful in the operation, when he wins, he wins graciously—he doesn't crow about it. And when he loses, and sometimes a real winner will lose one, he loses gracefully—he doesn't cry about it.

When he does lose and you say to him, "Why did you lose? You are supposed to be a real winner," he will look you squarely in the eye, put his hands on his hips, glare at the scoreboard and say, "I'll be damned if I know why we lost. We didn't plan to lose. We didn't practice to lose. We didn't play to lose. We used every ounce of our energy and every spark of our spirit all the way from the opening whistle to the final gun. The scoreboard says we got beat. Let me tell you something. We got beat on the scoreboard, but we did not get beat in the heart. We are still undefeated in the heart. And we'll be bouncing back upon that scoreboard. You can bet on that."

Well, you *can* bet on it, because every fiber of that kid's being vibrates with a powerful, positive punch which pounds always toward victory. It is natural for him to win. It is in his nature to win. He was brought up that way. He is a real winner. Ten percent of our people are real winners.

Take one of these guys we call a real loser and analyze him. When he goes forth to do something, he doesn't have the clear, vivid picture in his mind of the thing he is fighting for. He is not sure what he is fighting for. His picture is sort of messed up with shades of gray. He does not have the intense, burning desire in his heart to fight for it. He's not sure why he's bothering to fight at all. His desire is watered down with some other things. When he wins, he does not win graciously because he crows about it. He crows to high heaven. He puffs himself up and beats himself on the chest and he says, "Look me over, baby. I'm the hottest thing in town. I'm the winner. I'm the champ." When he loses, he does not lose gracefully because he cries about it.

When he does lose and you say to him, "Why did you lose? You had them outweighed. You should have won that one," he may look you squarely in the eye—the real loser does not necessarily lack courage, he lacks direction—and tell you exactly why he lost. "You saw old Joe out there. The clock was running out. We were one point behind. Old Joe was going down the sideline, wide open. You saw me throw that ball forty yards down that sideline. I put it one foot in front of old Joe's nose as he crossed over into the Promised Land. You saw old Joe drop it. The pistol went off. Old Joe lost the ball game."

Or it might be, "Fellow, look at this ankle. I got hurt in the first quarter of the game. Let's face facts. I'm the go-guy of this football team. I'm the bell-cow of the backfield. I score three times every game I play. I didn't score a single touchdown today. That old dog just wouldn't hunt out there today."

He might also say this: "You know why we lost? Just look at that old, baldheaded baboon that we've got for a coach. If you don't get rid of him, we are going to lose some more," or "You saw those guys in the striped shirts. Jesse James used a pistol. Those guys used a whistle. They poured the yellow rag to us all afternoon. We were robbed."

A real loser can always tell you exactly why he lost because he knows all the reasons for losing; therefore he is always prepared mentally and spiritually to lose. So he gets many, many losses. Don't bet on him. Every fiber of his being is saturated with alibi on top of alibi, which gets him ready to lose. It is his nature to lose. He is a real loser. That is 10 percent of our people.

Take one of the guys in the middle, the shoulder shrugger, and analyze him. When he goes forth to do something, he does not have a clear, vivid picture in his mind of the thing he's fighting for because it's just not that important. He does not have that intense, burning desire in his heart to fight for it. It's not *that* important. When he wins, he wins graciously enough because it's not important enough to get all puffed up over. When he loses, he loses gracefully enough because it's not important enough to get all hot and bothered about.

When he does lose and you say to him, "Why did you lose? You had more power. You should have won this one," he will look at you, smile sweetly, turn his hands palm up, *shrug his shoulders*, and say, "Oh, you know how it is; win a few, lose a few—that's life." And that *is* life to 80 percent of the American people, win a few, lose a few—ho, hum.

Here, boys, is the great fertile field for any man who occupies a position of leadership in this country, the 80 percent, the shoulder shruggers. Ten boys come to you to play football. One is a real winner. He will be your captain someday. One is a real loser. Get rid of him. He will get you fired. He will ruin your morale. He will lose you football games. Eight of the ten are shoulder shruggers. Here is the great fertile field for the football coach. The only difference between the real winner and a shoulder shrugger is this: The real winner has a clear vivid picture of what he is fighting for, and an intense, burning desire to fight for it. You must paint that picture, give the shoulder shrugger purpose, motivate his desire, reach his spirit. Motivation is the stuff that permeates mind, body, and soul toward the noble goal.

Coach, you are a leader of red-blooded youths. You must stir, you must stimulate, you must arouse, you must inspire until those young people are *eager* to rush out and fight the good fight.

Fighting the good fight was something Tiger had been programmed to do from his very early years, and he continued to exude that positive energy into his retirement years. He spent his morning hours working on manuscripts for two more books for coaches, and answering correspondence from young coaches about Run and Shoot. Some of those inquiries were now coming from Canada, Great Britain, Finland, and Germany. That was exciting! In the evenings, he would read, or watch sports and enjoy the evolution of the great game of American football.

But the afternoons were for play, and he took up golf with every intention of hitting par each time he stepped foot on a course. One of Sarasota's finest golf courses received twenty-one consecutive balls into the drink on one water hole because Tiger refused to stop trying to get it to the other side. He knew no other way. He was programmed to be a winner, and would never give up on the game until he reached the coveted goal of playing par golf a few years later. But of course, every golfer knows that you can't expect to make par every time; win some, lose some, right? Not for Tiger! *Expectation* comes by looking out and seeing the game from a bystander's perspective. *Intention* comes from seeing within and finding the will within your own heart. He intended to hit par or better every time. He had grown up a winner, and it was the only way he knew how to live.

When he saw his old friend Woody Hayes get himself into an altercation with a Clemson lad in the Gator Bowl in 1978, Tiger just shook his head. Not in disbelief, he knew the man's proclivity for striking out. He also knew that those raw fists pounding on fourteen pounds of pads were doing no harm to the boy. But sadly, it was an inglorious way for a great coach to exit the game. The politics of the powerhouse, however, would demand that action be taken. "Poor little lad. Big, mean, nasty coach," that was sort of how things had become by then.

Tiger and Woody corresponded over the next few years, but Woody seemed to have lost some of his positive energy that had made him such a warrior and determined winner. Then in the fall of 1983, Woody called.

He told me they wanted to honor him at halftime of the Homecoming Game, by having him dot the *i* in the beautiful *Script Ohio* that the band wrote out on special occasions. He said to me, "Fly up here and go out on the field with me, Tiger. You deserve it as much as I do." Well, I didn't believe that for one second. And Elsie had been dealing with some health issues that made travel difficult at that time.

But I sensed that my old friend needed some moral support, since this would be the first time he had set foot into the Horseshoe Stadium in five years. And I knew his love of the game would make this an emotional homecoming for him. So I said, "Woody, you know, Elsie and I were up there in Columbus for a speaking engagement in 1979. Do you remember that big old billboard on Olentangy River Road that the Jai Lai Restaurant always advertised on? Well, we drove by it, and there was your big ugly mug smiling down at us, and in huge print it said, 'IN ALL THE WORLD, THERE'S ONLY ONE.'

"Listen, buddy, it only takes one man to dot the *i* in *Script Ohio*, and you are the one they want to celebrate. Enjoy the moment! You deserve it, and the Buckeye Nation loves you!"

Well, it brought a little tear to my eye when I watched on TV as he went out on the field to get his just reward. I think I saw a little tear in Woody's eye too, when the loud, pulsating, standing ovation went on so long that they had to sort of usher him off the field so they could start the second half. A great tribute to a great coach. I know it had to mean a lot to him. He loved Ohio State, its football and its fans. I felt great joy that they still loved him, too.

Many things about men of this era would be difficult for the younger generation to understand. These guys grew up during a depression and a war pursued for the God-given right to be free. They believed down to their very fiber that freedom in America was not an automatic entitlement to a good life, and it certainly was not free. It was an opportunity preserved by the brave people who defended it, on every front and at every level of personal commitment. It was a chance and a choice to be exercised, by those with the personal will to win. Duty, honor, and country were words without need of verbal definition, but full of the spirit that required no explanation for them.

In his later years, Tiger would never understand how young people could be talking about tearing down the "Establishment," without regard for the pillars of truth and pursuit of ideals that men and women before them had sacrificed to preserve. Those pillars gave them the right to express their opinions, but he hoped to hear thoughts and ideas for how to improve what they didn't like about it, not just opinions for tearing it all down. Democratic societies are always messy and inefficient, struggling with their collective consciousness, particularly when they get off course. But if they measure their actions by those pillars of truth at their foundation, they will eventually self-correct.

Opinions seemed to Tiger like things foisted upon others, in order to sway them or impress them or get them to change. He found opinions a poor substitute for thoughtful, knowledgeable reflection that would frequently lead to deeper insight and more serious probing. *Pinions*, on the other hand, were the pillars of principle, timeless and universal, deeper truth that could take a whole lifetime of learning to understand in their finest form. Those pinions were the galvanizing strength of the American way that could not be denied, and would eventually correct any circumstances.

The game of life is a continuous learning process, and one can only play the game by cultivating an understanding of truth at its deepest level. As Bob Hart said, "The toughest measure of the man is how he used his winning spirit to play the game." Tiger often put it this way in his speeches.

Life is a game with a glorious prize,
If only we figure it right.
It's give and take, and build or break,
And often requires a fight.
But surely he wins who honestly tries,
Regardless of wealth or fame.
He'll never despair who plays it fair.
How are *you* playing the game?

Do you wilt and whine if you fail to win
In a manner you think your due?
Do you sneer at the man who honestly can,
And does, do better than you?
Or do you take rebuffs with a knowing grin,
And laugh when you pull up lame?
Does your faith hold true when you'd rather feel blue?
How are *you* playing the game?

Jump into the thick of it all, my friend,
Whatever your cherished goal.
Brace up with your will till your pulses thrill,
And you dare with your very soul!
Do something more than make chattering noise;
Let your purpose leap into the flame.
As you plunge forward, cry "I shall do it or die!"
Then *you'll* be playing the game.[19]

---

[19] Author unknown

15

THE BRIDGE BUILDER

Tiger Ellison was not a man who sought accolades for his work. Excellence was, after all, its own reward. He was first and foremost a teacher, and he thought the gridiron of American football was the greatest setting of all for teaching young people the fundamentals of sportsmanship, confidence, courage, and teamwork, all focused on a shared and worthy goal, and all characteristics required for living a successful and fulfilling life under America's democratic principles.

Tiger would never invest his spirit into putting another person down, or insult him by feeling sorry for him. He would only invest in finding the best the person had in him, and then spend his energies trying to inspire and motivate it. He believed down to his very core that each person has a "Quarterback Within" that must call the game based on the situation he or she is faced with, cope with the consequences of those decisions, get up and back in the game when knocked down, learn from the things that didn't work, and become better at the things that did. Preparation, practice, and play in the game of life gave noble purpose to a man's fighting spirit, both for the quarterback within and the team around him.

Not everyone Tiger taught and coached was prepared to accept that personal responsibility. But Tiger believed he could not help a person who was not willing and determined to take ownership of his personal path and apply his fighting spirit to the game of life. For Tiger, this was a personal philosophy for living that was a certainty of belief, and it was the only way he knew.

He lived those principles from the time he was a boy throughout his life, paying forward to those who followed behind him. His love of life, country, and sport were contagious. But inevitably, as age caught up with him and his mortal body began to give up ground, his American fighting spirit got another calling, one he could not ignore.

As he lay in the hospital bed, the light dimming in the pale blue eyes, he murmured to his daughter, "I'm an old man, going a lone highway." Her baby blues twinkled back at him, "You'll never be alone, Tiger. You've built too many bridges for others to follow." And then she quietly recited to him his favorite story that he had so often propounded from the podium as he spoke to coaches and young people about their responsibilities for building boys and molding men:

>**An old man, going a lone highway,**
>**Came in the evening, cold and gray,**
>**To a chasm, vast and deep and wide,**
>**Through which was flowing a sullen tide.**
>**The old man crossed in the twilight dim.**
>**That swollen stream held no fears for him.**
>**But he paused when safe on the other side,**
>**And he built a bridge to span the tide.**
>
>**"Old man," said a fellow traveler near,**
>**"You're wasting strength with building here.**
>**"Your journey will end with the ending day,**
>**"And you never again must pass this way.**
>**"You've crossed the chasm, deep and wide,**
>**"Why build you a bridge at the even' tide?"**
>
>**The builder lifted his old gray head,**
>**"Good friend, in the path I've come," he said,**
>**"There follows after me today**
>**"A youth whose feet must pass this way.**
>**"That swollen stream, which was naught to me,**
>**"To that wholesome lad may a pitfall be.**
>**"He, too, must cross in the twilight dim.**
>**"Good friend, I am building the bridge for him."**[20]

AAAAAY, Go, Tiger man.

---

[20] Will Allen Dromgoole, "The Bridge Builder," circa 1900

Afterword

FOOTPRINTS ON THE BRIDGE

Rocko Joslin, MHS, Class of '50: If I had not run across Tiger Ellison for high school football, I probably would have been satisfied to pack my lunch pail every day and head off to the Armco Machine Shop like my dad did. But Tiger challenged me to apply myself to college prep studies, and after earning a football scholarship and graduating from Ohio State, I started work at Armco instead as an industrial engineer in Butler, Pennsylvania. One of my early responsibilities was to head up union negotiations, and the labor leaders told me I was always tough, but always fair. I liked that, and believe that's what football can teach you. In Butler, I started a Pop Warner Little League and taught hundreds of young boys the lessons I learned on the gridiron of Middletown High School. I retired from Armco as director of operations in Ashland, Kentucky. It was a great run, influenced by a great coach and motivator.

Bob Grimes, MHS, Class of '49: Some twenty years after I had graduated from high school, I attended a professional seminar in which the speaker had a good idea for us. He passed out postcards and suggested we send a note to someone who had had a positive influence in our lives. Giving forward is a great idea, but it never hurts to remember to give thanks back to those who motivated us along the way. I went home and, without hesitation, jotted my note of gratitude to Tiger for his inspiring philosophy and its positive impact on my life. He was unforgettable.

Joe Galat, Co-Founder of American Youth Football, Inc.; Former Head Coach and General Manager, Montreal Alouettes and BC Lions of the Canadian Football League: I first heard of Tiger Ellison when I was a football player at Miami University, and my good friend and teammate, Bob Hart, and I were discussing the influence a great high school coach had on each of our lives. We went over to Middletown to watch one of Tiger's games, and the announcer from the press box passed along some Tiger philosophy: "These boys out here tonight wear their school colors proudly, and while they may get a little bark scraped off their noses, they are learning from football how to be a red-blooded American!" Then we watched this Run and Shoot offense that he had created, and it was the most innovative and exciting thing I had ever seen! There is no doubt in my mind that it changed the game forever once he published his book on *Run and Shoot Football: Offense of the Future.* It has since morphed into the West Coast Offense.

As a young coach, a couple years later, I came to understand the man better when he made a luncheon speech at the AFCA annual convention in New York. Now, coaches as a lot don't sit easily in chairs for long periods of time, and the banquet was noisy and distracting, with old friends shouting across tables at each other and dishes clanging as lunches were being inhaled. Tiger walked to the podium, took off his sport coat, and began a story about "The Old Man of the Desert." After about the second sentence, something happened that I had never experienced before. Silence! Thousands of coaches from the head table to the ones near the exits sat attentively in awe of this man for the next forty-five minutes! I can still recall the moral of his story: "Show me a classroom in this country where you can sit a kid at a desk and teach him confidence, courage, teamwork, and leadership, like you can on the gridiron of American football."

I heard later that General Douglas MacArthur, who was to be our keynote speaker in the evening, had stuck his head into the meeting room just as Tiger began his speech, and ended up staying for the whole thing. Afterward, he went up to the podium, and as he shook Tiger's hand, he said, "Coach, the next time we appear on the dais together, you make sure I go first!" What a great compliment!

Gary Getter, MHS Class of '56, Senior Co-Captain: I revered Tiger Ellison and wanted to follow in his footsteps as a coach and teacher. What I found after a couple years in the school system was that I was more cut out to work with adults than with youngsters. So I began a thirty-year career in Human Resource Management with Armco, getting people to work together toward a common goal, building teamwork, improving skills, pushing them to produce and become the best they could be. The fundamentals of coaching were still at the heart of everything I did professionally. Football under a great, inspiring coach like Tiger teaches lessons for life on any arena where people need to be working together.

Jan Knepshield, MHS Class of '59, Senior Co-Captain: Tiger Ellison was one of the great stalwarts of the teaching and coaching professions, and the reason I chose them as my own career for thirty-nine years. I co-captained the team that year he created the Lonesome Polecat, and man, did we have fun with that the second half of the season! Knowing what was behind it and how it evolved to his Run and Shoot offense, there is no doubt in my mind that Tiger's innovations were behind what is known today as the West Coast Offense. He was way ahead of his times. I will be forever grateful to have known the man.

Jim Place, Former Head Coach, Middletown High School: Tiger was an outstanding coach, educator, community leader, and a true role model for every other coach. But the attribute that struck me most was his gift for motivational speaking. When Tiger told a story, the vivid pictures of events were so real that you felt you were right there in the action, and later you could replay them over and over again. He would move back and forth as he spoke, making eye contact and pointing to one young person at a time, calling him "Man" or some other flattering name to a youngster. By the time he was finished, every single person in the audience felt personally connected to him.

I first heard of Tiger as a young, wide-eyed, twenty-two-year-old coach attending my first Ohio State Clinic. I left with visions of Rocko Joslin pounding on the coach's door, and other Tiger favorites. Little did I know that years later, I would be entrusted with carrying on his legacy as head coach of his beloved Middies. I never missed an opportunity to tell the team about the great Tiger Ellison and his players. We would speak of the tradition they had passed on to them, not only of winning, but also doing everything first class.

Jim Otis, OSU Class of '70, 1968 National Champ: I can always remember when we got into training camp my freshman year and saw Tiger. Here was this old man and here we were, young guys full of lots of energy and enthusiasm. How tough could this be, right? Well, he ran us into the ground! We couldn't keep up with him, on either the energy or enthusiasm scale! He was quite a guy.[21]

---

[21] *Buckeye Sports Bulletin* 9, no. 30 (August 1990)

Dr. Rex Kern, OSU Class of '71, 1968 National Champ and 1969 Rose Bowl MVP: What a wonderful time it was to be a Buckeye when I was an undergraduate! Tiger was one of those magical characters that inspired and loved us. And we loved him back so very much. He was way ahead of his time as far as offensive football was concerned. But what made him so remarkable was his passion for life, country, and sport that were absolutely contagious for those around him. When you read his story, you may laugh a little, (or a lot, which may bring you to tears!), you may learn some things about football strategy, but most of all I am certain you will learn to love Tiger and his positive philosophy of life as much as we did!

Earle Bruce, Former Head Coach, Ohio State University: In life you meet people who stand out in your mind as good teachers, good communicators, great leaders, and wonderful role models for our young people. Tiger Ellison was number one in all these achievements. He was a shining example to all of us, and I hope that every teacher, coach, and player who has read this story will reconnect with the purpose of our honorable profession and the great sport of American football. Tiger Ellison, you surely did walk tall and straight with this coach.

Bibliography

Glenn "Tiger" Ellison. *Run and Shoot Football: Offense of the Future.* West Nyack, NY: Parker Publishing Company, 1965.

Glenn "Tiger" Ellison. *Run and Shoot Football: The Now Attack.* West Nyack, NY: Parker Publishing Company, 1984.

Glenn "Tiger" Ellison. *Tiger Ellison's Secrets of Persuasive Speaking for Coaches.* West Nyack, NY: Parker Publishing Company, 1966.

Glenn "Tiger" Ellison. *Power Speaking that Gets Results.* West Nyack, NY: Parker Publishing Company, 1974.

American Football Coaches Association. *The Football Coaching Bible.* Champaign, IL: Human Kinetics, 2002.

American Football Coaches Association. *Football Offenses & Plays.* Champaign, IL: Human Kinetics, 2006.

Tom Flores, Bob O'Conner. *Coaching Football.* Chicago, IL: Masters Press, 1993.

Al Black. *Coaching Run-and-Shoot Football.* Haworth, NJ: Harding Press, 1991.

Ron Jenkins. *Coaching the Multiple West Coast Offense*, Second Edition. Monterey, CA: Coaches Choice, 2003.

Jim Tressel. *What It Means To Be a Buckeye*, Edited by Jeff Snook. Chicago: Triumph Books, 2003.

Lou Holtz. *Wins, Losses, and Lessons*. NY: William Morrow, HarperCollins Publishers, 2006.

Steve Greenberg, Larry Zelina. *Ohio State '68: All the Way to the Top*. Champaign, IL: Sports Publishing, 1998.

Michael MacCambridge. *America's Game*. NY: Random House, 2004.

John M. Barry. *Rising Tide*. NY: Touchstone, 1997.

William A. Hamm. *From Colony to World Power*. Boston: D. C. Heath and Company, 1947.

Theodora Lau. *The Handbook of Chinese Horoscopes*, Fourth Edition. NY: HarperCollins Publishers, 2000.

Suzanne Mettler. *Soldiers to Citizens*. NY: Oxford University Press, 2005.

Made in the USA
Lexington, KY
06 June 2015